UNDERSTANDING JAPAN
Through the Eyes of Christian Faith

UNDERSTANDING JAPAN
Through the Eyes of Christian Faith

Third Edition

SAMUEL LEE, PHD

Copyright 2009 by Dr. Samuel Lee

Published by Foundation University Press
Verrijn Stuartweg 31, Diemen 1112 AW, The Netherlands

www.foundationuniversity.com

This book or parts thereof may not be reproduced in any form, stored in a retrieval system or transmitted in any form by any means-electronic, mechanical, photocopy, recording or otherwise- without prior written permission of the publisher, except as provided by the European Copyright Law and United States of America Copyright Law.

ISBN: 978-94-90179-01-4

Copyright © 2009 by Foundation University Press

*This work is dedicated to
my beloved family*

"In 1597 the blood of the martyrs was shed on the hills of Nagasaki. The incident in this dissertation is very impressive. Before the execution with other 25 Christians, a 12 year old boy, Ludvico Ibaragi told the officer who begged him to recant his faith, 'Sir, it would be better if you yourself became a Christian and could go to heaven where I am going. Sir, which is my cross?'

I can sense through this book that Dr. Samuel Lee has a deep concern for Japan and the Japanese people with God's love.

His view of Japan is not stereotyped. He acknowledges the elements in the Japanese culture that are hindering Japanese believers from sharing the gospel to others. He indicates that Kumi consisted of five or more households were obligated to report any hidden Christians to the authorities in Tokugawa period as one of the organized persecutions to the Christians.

His analysis, in relation with the Japanese cultural stronghold, of the concept of Honne-Tatemae or Uchi-Soto, on hindering the churches to grow is very keen and gives us distinguished strategies to reach Japan with the gospel. He reveals the social-cultural illness, such as high rate of suicide, Hikikomori and Free-tar and challenges the churches in Japan to open the doors to them accepting them and solving their problems.

Dr. Lee challenges us to provide biblical and ethical solutions for the Japanese men and women who are undergoing radical social, economical and cultural changes and are searching new things.

After reading through this book I can not help but make up my mind to rededicate myself to give them the answer to show the living and loving Father, for whom Ludvico Ibaragi exchanged his life.

I pray that this book will be the mighty trigger for the churches in Japan to break down the cultural stronghold and reach the suffering people with the gospel as never before."

Pastor Hiroko Ayabe
Founder, Japan Revival Ministries
Tama Gospel Center

"I highly recommend this insightful new book from Samuel Lee. He accurately assesses the major cultural and historical barriers to Christianity that have been built into Japanese society, and offers thoughtful strategies for breaking those barriers down. This book will be an asset to anyone who has a heart for Japan and longs to see it transformed."

Rev. Ron Sawka,
President, Christian International Asia Tochigi Japan

"Japan is a nation ready for the Gospel. However, for decades there has been a missing piece to the missiological puzzle. Samuel Lee's profound book is a giant step toward revealing that missing piece. Once it is uncovered and applied, Japan will experience the bountiful spiritual harvest we have been waiting for!"

C. Peter Wagner, PhD
Chancellor, Wagner Leadership Institute

"Dr. Samuel Lee presents a thorough treatment of Japanese history and society from a Christian perspective. His analysis is helpful for Western Christians who are interested in investigating the factors hindering their effective witness in Japan."

Rev. Mike Wilson
Asian Access Okinawa Japan

"Samuel Lee has combined brilliant research and deep spiritual insights to produce a landmark work of scholarship on the spiritual forces that have shaped the nation of Japan. He has made a valuable contribution to the missions' community by unlocking the secrets of a society that has been closed to the rest of the world for centuries. This book provides the global church with a valuable key to opening and reaching Japan with the gospel."

J. Lee Grady
Senior Editor, Charisma Magazine

CONTENTS

Preface — xv

Methodology — xix

Part One — JAPAN — A BRIEF REVIEW — 1

Chapter 1 — The Origin of the Japanese People — 3

Chapter 2 — The History of Japan — 13

Part Two — JAPANESE SOCIETY — 29

Chapter 3 — The Japanese Family — 33

Chapter 4 — Japanese Working Life — 43

Chapter 5 — Social Stratification in Japan — 49

Part Three — CHRISTIANITY IN JAPAN — 63

Chapter 6 — Main Religions in Japan — 67

Chapter 7 — The History of Christianity in Japan — 77

Chapter 8 — Christianity in Japan Today — 91

Part Four	**JAPANESE CULTURE & CHRISTIAN FAITH**	95
Chapter 9	Christianity Defined	99
Chapter 10	Elements of Japanese Culture	105
Chapter 11	Spiritual Culture in Japan	121
Chapter 12	Socio-Cultural Illness	127
Part Five	**CONCLUSIONS AND ANALYSIS**	141
Chapter 13	Analyses and Strategies	143
Bibliography		155

"My people would not immediately become Christians, but they would first ask you a multitude of questions, weighing carefully your answers and your claims. Above all, they would observe whether your conduct agrees with your words. If you should satisfy them on these points by suitable replies to their inquiries and by a life above reproach, then, as soon as the matter was known and fully examined, the king, the nobles, and the educated people would become Christians. Six months would suffice; for the nation is one that always follows the guidance of reason."

— Anjiro, 1548

PREFACE

Understanding the Japanese culture and society has attracted many scholars. Many have desired to research and write about this fascinating nation. Some have various ideas and have developed many theories about Japan and how to analyze and deal with this culture. I have always been intrigued by the Japanese culture. While studying sociology at the University of Leiden in the Netherlands I chose Japan as my regional specialization.

Whether we are conscious about it or not, the Japanese culture is already making its mark on the global culture. It is advancing in a very unique and rapid way, penetrating almost every part of the world. Not only has Japan captured the global markets with her cars and electronics, but now she is also conquering the world with her Manga-culture and Japanese animation personalities. This includes games, films, cartoons, and the entire commerce around them. One time, while I was in a village in South Africa, I was surprised when I saw that children were already exposed to Japanese cartoons and animations such as Pokémon and Digimon! Japanese cartoons and animation personalities are often influenced by thousands of years of Japanese mythology and culture. They are being transformed and adapted into the modern twenty-first century culture.

Japanese society is extremely westernized. At times it is much more westernized than the West itself. The Japanese people are excellent in adopting an imported lifestyle, and they make it their own while adopting it with their cultural elements. Once a professor in Japanese sociology said, "Japanese people are more American than Americans themselves." While the western lifestyle has been very well established and adopted into Japanese culture, the Christian faith only has two percent of the population. Why is Christianity not widely accepted in Japan and what can Christians do to change this situation? There are various reasons. In this book I am seeking answers to these very important questions. How should the Christian faith approach Japan in such a way that Christianity can expand in this nation? Seeing the recent developments of the Japanese society, I believe it is now the right time to address this issue.

Japanese society is on the verge of many new things. While the youth have all they need materially, there are things they lack both spiritually and mentally. There is a high rate of suicide among the youth in Japan. There are websites that are helping people, young and old, to commit suicide. The main reason for this is loneliness. While everyone is busy with work and life, the children, youth, women and elderly are being neglected. Japan is a nation with great Christian potential. People are searching. They are looking for answers, and I believe this is the right time for Christianity to be preached in this nation.

The Japanese are a very productive people. If they can promote their products in such an excellent and rapid way, such as they did in the years after World War II, how much more can the Japanese Christians do the same with the gospel of Jesus Christ? But why are Japanese Christians unable to effectively spread the Christian faith? One of the reasons is that there are elements in the Japanese culture that are hindering Japanese believers from openly speaking about the gospel to others. In this book I will be exploring some of these Japanese cultural elements and try to explain how these elements can be used to advance the gospel in Japan.

When Japan becomes an exporter of Christianity along with its technology and science, the gospel will rapidly expand not only in Asia but also all around the world! We have to motivate and encourage the Japanese believers to do this. That is why it is very important to invest in Japanese Christianity and to witness effectively to the Japanese people. In order to invest in Japan and prepare this nation for the gospel of Christ, we have to understand the Japanese culture. This includes their way of thinking, their society, and the functioning of Japan's social structures. In this dissertation,

I will be looking at the cultural elements of Japanese society that are potential cultural gateways for reaching the Japanese for Christ. I will also examine the hindrances for taking the gospel to this nation.

In Part One, I will be sketching a review of Japan as a nation both in the past and today. Japanese history will be discussed briefly. In Part Two, I will be dealing with important elements of the Japanese society including gender relationships, family relations, and economic aspects. In Part Three, Christianity in Japan will be described. This includes the history and the present condition of the Christian faith in this nation. I will define the general history of Christianity and her developments in globalization in Asia. Then I will turn to Japan and discuss Japanese Christianity in particular. At the same time, the general condition of religion in Japan will be described. In particular, I will focus on Buddhism, Shinto, and Confucianism. In Part Four, I will be discussing the Japanese culture in regard to the gospel. I will be bringing the previous chapters together and analyzing what has been discussed. I will then look at the various cultural barriers and hindrances. In regard to cultural barriers, I will be looking at the elements that I believe are hindrances for the gospel to be accepted in Japan. Then I will be giving suggestions concerning how to approach the Japanese people in order to get the gospel to them. In Part Five, conclusions and future perspectives will be discussed. Advice will be given, and I will be looking for solutions to bring the gospel to Japan in a proper and strategic way.

METHODOLOGY

I have researched various articles, magazines, and books. The Internet also has been a great help for accumulating information. I humbly must warn the reader that this book is not objective. This book is written in the context of my Christian worldview, and the purpose of this book is to understand Japan through the eyes of Christian faith so that this book will be used as a handbook to foreign missionaries and people who are interested in Japan and interceding for Japan from a Christian point of view.

Part One
JAPAN — A BRIEF REVIEW

CHAPTER

THE ORIGIN OF THE JAPANESE PEOPLE

INTRODUCTION

Japan is an exciting nation in our modern world today. This old country with inhabitants of approximately 120 million people is one of the important economic powers in Asia and the world. After World War II and her defeat by the allied forces, Japan was a ruined nation because of nuclear bombardments, poverty, and chaos. However, after fifty years Japan has become a leader in economics, technology, the arts, science, sports, and politics.

Post-World War II Asian nations, even though they were affected by Japanese aggression, still choose the Japanese way of development.

How did it start and where is the root of such development? The answer to this complicated question may be found in the historical development of Japan, the development of her culture, and the evolution of Japanese society throughout different eras. Before looking into the historical aspects, here is some basic information on the geographical setting of Japan.

Japan is made of four main islands and some 3900 little islands. These collections of islands begin from the north Soya down to the south near Taiwan. The four main islands of Japan are from north to south — Hokkaido, Honshu, Shikoku, and Kyushu.

Tokyo, the capital city, and some other important cities like Osaka, Kobe, and Yokohama, are on Honshu Island, the largest island of Japan. Nagasaki is situated in Kyushu. Japan is divided into forty-seven prefectures which are equivalent to states or provinces in other countries. The closest neighboring countries to Japan are Russia from the north and North Korea and South Korea from the west.

There have been difficulties with neighboring countries concerning the territorial boundaries of Japan. This involves some islands that are claimed both by the Japanese and Russians or by the Japanese and Koreans.

The earliest Japanese historical period is the Jomon Period dating approximately from 8000 B.C. until 300 B.C. The Jomons were remarkable pottery makers. Many believe that gradually the Jomon people moved northward.

There are various theories and mythological beliefs concerning the origin of the Japanese people. Some believe that the Jomons were the first inhabitants of Japan. Some link the Japanese origin to the Tungus people of the North. The Tungus are a Siberian ethnic group numbering perhaps 30,000 today. They are subdivided into the Evenki who live in the area from the Yenisei and Ob river basins to the Pacific Ocean, and from the Amur River to the Arctic Ocean, and the Lamut who live on the coast of the Okhotsk Sea. The Tungus are closely related to the Manchus. Before they were brought under Soviet control the Tungus practiced a shamanistic religion. The Tungus and Tunguzic languages are a division of the Altaic subfamily of the Ural-Altaic family of languages that includes the Manchu literary language; they may be related to those who are Mongolic and Turkic.

Some also believe that the Japanese people find their origin in the Austronesian people from South Asia. Countries such as Indonesia and the Philippines are examples of Austronesian people. Some others believe that their origin may be a mixture of both the Tungus and Austronesian people.

Another interesting theory is that the Japanese people come from one of the lost tribes of Israel. After discussing the mythological origin of Japan, I will be discussing the "Israel-Japan" theory that is relevant to this research.

MYTHOLOGICAL ORIGINS

"Mythological origins" means what the Japanese believe to be the formation of Japan as a nation and people. Since this is a myth it may not have scientific evidence. Yet it is crucial for it certainly has cultural value which may influence the way the Japanese people look at their nation and themselves. Therefore, I will discuss this mythology on the formation of Japan.

This is how the myth goes: Ground was born only when it was flossy like the oil that floats on water. The god, Izanagi, and the goddess, Izanami, looked down on the ground from a very high place on the sky to harden the ground and make a good country. The two inserted a long halberd into the sea to harden the ground and to make a country. They stirred it with rolling. The seawater that fell from the tip of the halberd accumulated fast and became the island.

The two who saw this were pleased and descended on this island and married. After that they gave birth to the islands: Shikoku, Honshu, Kyushu, etc. The country of Japan was born in this way. After the god, Izanagi, married the goddess, Izanami, they begot a son named Susanoonomikoto (Susanowo) with the daughter named Amaterasuoomikami (Amaterasu). Amaterasu is the Japanese Shinto sun goddess, ruler of the Plain of Heaven, whose name means "shining heaven" or "she who shines in the heavens." She is the central figure in the Shinto pantheon, and the Japanese imperial family claims its descent from her. She is the eldest daughter of Izanagi. She was so bright and radiant that her parents sent her up the Celestial Ladder to heaven where she has ruled ever since. When her brother, the storm-god, Susanowo, ravaged the earth, Amaterasu retreated to a cave because her brother was so noisy. She closed the cave with a large boulder. Her disappearance deprived the world of light and life. Demons ruled the earth. The other gods used everything in their power to lure her out but to no avail. Finally it was Uzume who succeeded. The laughter of the gods, when they watched her comical and obscene dances, aroused Amaterasu's curiosity.

When she emerged from her cave a streak of light escaped. The goddess then saw her own brilliant reflection in a mirror, which Uzume had hung in a nearby tree. When she drew closer for a better look, the gods grabbed her and pulled her out of the cave. She returned to the sky and brought light back into the world.

Later, she created rice fields called inada where she cultivated rice. She also invented the art of weaving with the loom and taught the people how to cultivate wheat and silkworms.

Amaterasu's main sanctuary is Ise-Jingue situated on Ise on the island of Honshu. This temple is pulled down every twenty years and then rebuilt in its original form. In the inner sanctum she is represented by a mirror (her body). She is also called Omikami, meaning "illustrious goddess."

What was just mentioned above indicates that the Japanese people believe, or at least many believe, that Japan is a divine nation according to Shinto belief. This may influence how they look at the nation and how they behave and relate to other things. This type of thinking was very well promoted in the Meiji Period (1868–1912) in Japanese history. Later I will describe this era.

ISRAEL — JAPAN THEORY

Recently, certain scientists, theologians, historians, and cultural anthropologists have discovered what they believe is the origin of the Japanese people. They claim that the Japanese people are the offspring of the tribes of Israel going back to approximately 700 B.C. The story goes back to the time when Israel was divided into parts, the Northern kingdom, which was called Israel, and the Southern kingdom, which was called Judah.

The Northern kingdom, Israel, was made of ten tribes and the Southern kingdom of two tribes — Judah and Benjamin.

In 722 B.C., the Assyrians attacked the Northern kingdom which was ruled by King Hoshea who took the Israelites, the ten tribes, into exile. The Assyrian king replaced the Jews and spread them to various locations.

There is some evidence that the Jews gradually traveled through the Silk Road and went as far away as Japan. The ancient book of history, the fourth book of Ezra, which is not a canonical book, says that the ten tribes of the Northern kingdom of Israel went east and walked for one and a half years to a far away land. They moved through Afghanistan. Some went through

Kashmir, India, and some parts of China and Japan. There are strong evidences of Jewish customs in these nations. For instance, the Afghan people are also called "Bani Israel," which means "children of Israel."

The Bible also says, in Isaiah 11:12: "He (God)...will assemble the outcasts of Israel, and gather together the dispersed of Judah from the four corners of the earth." According to a Chinese historical book, there were Israelites who had the custom of circumcision in the time of the second century B.C. in China. The ten tribes of Israel must have moved east passing through these countries. We cannot say there is no possibility that the main body of the ten tribes of Israel came far away to Japan. According to this theory, the lost tribes came to Japan in the early formation of the nation's history. Their religion and customs may have influenced the Shinto religion and the Japanese culture at that time. In ancient times, some people moved to Japan from China. Some people also came from Russia and some people from Southeast Asia. Among them, there is a possibility that the main body of the ten lost tribes of Israel also came to Japan. According to the research of Dr. Kawamorita, there appears God's holy name, "Yahweh," many times in ancient Japanese folk songs. The Jews of Judah do not use His name because they quit pronouncing His name after the third century B.C. Contrary to Judah, the people of Israel continued to pronounce His name.

The formal name for the emperor, "Jinmu," the first emperor of Japan, is "Kamu-yamato-iware-biko-sumera-mikoto." Joseph Eidelberg says that it can be interpreted in Hebrew as "The king of Samaria, the noble founder of the Hebrew nation of Yahweh." This is not to mean that "Jinmu" himself is really the founder of the Hebrew nation, but the memory of the Hebrew nation might have come into the legend of the Japanese first emperor, "Jinmu" (Kubo, 1999).

ISRAEL–JAPAN THEORY'S CULTURAL EVIDENCE

Arimasa Kubo, a Japanese writer and scholar, has gathered certain Japanese cultural ceremonies which he uses as proof to back up the Israel–Japan theory.

Here are some of these ceremonies which he has discussed in his book:

1. Ontosai Festival — Isaac Story
2. Shinto Shrine of Imperial House of Japan — Star of David
3. Yamabushi-Clothing, Japanese Priests in Training — Jewish Priests' Clothing
4. Omikoshi — the Ark of the Covenant
5. Shinto Shrine — Tabernacle of Ancient Israel
6. Ancient Japanese People and Yahweh (Jehovah)

There are many other elements that are interesting but not so relevant to this book.

Ontosai Festival — Isaac Story

According to Arimasa Kubo, there is a link between the Ontosai festival and the story of Isaac when Abraham took his son Isaac for a sacrifice, and the angel of the Lord stopped him and provided a ram to be sacrificed in Isaac's place.

In the Nagano prefecture in Japan, there is a large Shinto shrine named "Suwa-Taisha" (Shinto is the traditional religion peculiar to Japan). At Suwa-Taisha the traditional festival called Ontosai is held on April 15 every year. This festival illustrates the story of Isaac in Genesis 22 in the Bible. This describes the story of Abraham who was about to sacrifice his own son — Isaac in the region of Moraiah.

The festival, Ontosai, has been held since ancient days and has been thought of as the most important festival of Suwa-Taisha. Next to the shrine, Suwa-Taisha, there is a mountain called Mt. Moriya ("Moriya-san" in Japanese). And the people from the Suwa area call the god of Mt. Moriya "Moriya no kami" which means "the god of Moriya." At the festival, a boy is tied up by a rope to a wooden pillar and placed on a bamboo carpet.

A Shinto priest comes to him preparing a knife, but then a messenger (another priest) comes there and the boy is released. It reminds us of how

Isaac was released after an angel came to Abraham. At this festival, animal sacrifices are also offered; seventy-five deer are sacrificed, but among them it is believed that there is a deer with its ears split. The deer is believed to be the one that the god prepared. It may have some connection with the ram that God prepared and was sacrificed after Isaac was released. Even in historic times, people thought that this custom of deer sacrifice was strange because animal sacrifice is not a Shinto tradition.

People call this festival "the festival for Misakuchi-god." Misakuchi might be "mi-isaku-chi." "Mi" means "great." "Isaku" is probably Isaac (the Hebrew word "Yitzhak"), and "chi" is something for the end of the word.

It seems that the people of Suwa made Isaac a god probably by the influence of idol worshipers. Today, this custom of the boy about to be sacrificed and then released is no longer practiced, but we can still see the custom of the wooden pillar called "oniye-basira" which means "sacrifice-pillar" (Kubo, 1999).

Shinto Shrine of Imperial House of Japan — Star of David

Ise-jingu in the Mie-prefecture is the Shinto shrine built for the Imperial House of Japan. On both sides of the approaches to the shrine there are street lamps made of stone where the Jewish Star of David is carved on each of the lamps near the top. The crest of the Star of David is also used on the inside of the shrine (Izawa-no-miya) at Ise-jingu, which has been there since ancient times. In the Kyoto prefecture, there is a shrine called "Manai-jinja" which was the original Ise-jingu Shrine. The crest of "Manai-jinja" is also the Star of David which has been used since ancient times.

Yamabushi-Clothing, Japanese Priests in Training — Jewish Priests' Clothing

"Yamabushis" are religious men in training who are unique to Japan. Today, they are thought to belong to Japanese Buddhism. But the Buddhism in China, Korea, and India has no such custom.

The custom of "yamabushi" has existed in Japan before Buddhism was imported into Japan in the seventh century. The clothes worn by the "yamabushi" are basically white. On his forehead, he puts a black small box called a "tokin" which is tied to his head with a black cord. He really resembles a Jew putting on a phylactery (black box) on his forehead with a black cord.

The size of this black box "tokin" is almost the same as the Jewish phylactery. But the shape of the "tokin" is round and looks like a flower. Originally, the Jewish phylactery placed on the forehead seems to have come from the forehead "plate" put on the high priest Aaron with a cord (Exodus 28:36–38). It was about four centimeters (1.6 inches) in size according to folklore, and some scholars say that this was in the shape of a flower. If so, it was very similar to the shape of the Japanese tokin worn by the yamabushi.

Omikoshi — the Ark of Covenant

Arimasa Kubo indicates that the Japanese Omikoshi, which is being carried in festivals on their shoulders with poles, represents the Jewish priests carrying the ark of God in ancient Israel.

Shinto Shrine — Tabernacle of Ancient Israel

The tabernacle of God in ancient Israel was divided into two parts: the Holy Place and the Most Holy Place. According to Arimasa Kubo, the Shinto shrine is also divided in two parts, and the functions prepared in the Japanese shrine are similar to the ones of the Israeli tabernacle. Even the customs and rituals surrounding the Shinto shrine resemble Israel's ancient rituals in the Tabernacle. Just like the Jewish law and rules, the Japanese cannot enter inside the Holy Place. Only Shinto priests can enter. Shinto priests enter the "Holy of Holies" only at special times. This is the same as the Israeli tabernacle. The "Holy of Holies" of the Japanese Shinto shrines is located in the far west as in the Israeli tabernacle. Shinto's "Holy of Holies" is also located on a higher level than the "Holy Place" and between them there are steps. Scholars say that in the Israeli temple built by Solomon, the Holy of

Holies was on an elevated level as well, and between them there were steps of about 2.7 meters (9 feet) wide. In front of a Japanese shrine, there are two statues of lions called "komainu" that sit on both sides of the approach. They are not idols but guards for the shrine. This is also a custom of ancient Israel. In God's temple in Israel and in the palace of Solomon, there were statues or relieves of lions (1 Kings 7:36, 10:19). In the early history of Japan there were absolutely no lions. But the statues of lions have been placed in Japanese shrines since ancient times. It has been proven by scholars that statues of lions located in front of Japanese shrines originated from the Middle East. There are more rituals resembling the tabernacle rituals and Kubo describes them more in detail.

Ancient Japanese People and Yahweh (Jehovah)

There is a difference in that; the Shinto religion believes in many gods while the Israeli (Jewish) religion believes in only one true God. However, the ten lost tribes of Israel were also inclined to idol worship and polytheistic belief. They believed in the true God, Yahweh, but also Baal, Asytaroth, Molech, and other pagan gods. That is why, according the Bible, God's anger arose against the Israelites. Practically, the religion of ancient Israel was not monotheistic because they disobeyed the commands of Lord. Shinto's polytheistic belief seems to have come from the polytheistic inclination of ancient Israel. Shinto scholars say that a Shinto god, Susanoh, resembles Baal in several aspects, and a female Shinto god, Amaterasu, resembles Asytaroth.

Israel–Japan Theory — Conclusions

Clearly, the Shinto belief is not equal to the original Jewish faith, yet there are similarities that may indicate the movements of ten tribes of Israel to different parts of the Middle East, Central and Far Asia, and also Japan. Assuming that this theory may be true, we can conclude that the Jews entered Japan during the very early formation of this nation and the formation of the Shinto belief and Japanese culture. This means that the Israeli customs and rituals were easily received and adopted within the formation of the new nation and new culture of ancient Japan.

In this way Shinto belief, which was also in her formation, adopted not only the Israeli–Mosaic customs, but also the pagan customs of Baal and the worship of other gods. Since Shinto belief was a polytheistic belief, they had no problem adding more gods in their religious system.

CHAPTER 2

THE HISTORY OF JAPAN

THE ARISTOCRATIC AND FEUDAL AGE

As I mentioned earlier, Japanese history is believed to have started with the Jomon Period that started about eight thousand years before Christ. About this period we do not know much; we only know that the people of this era were pottery makers.

The Chinese chronicles mention the earliest historical registration of the Japanese people. According to these chronicles, there was a nation with one hundred kingdoms, whereby thirty of them sent envoys to China for business relationships.

According to these chronicles, there were continuous fights between these kingdoms, and a queen called Himiko then ruled a kingdom called Yamatai. She gained power over the other kingdoms. This all took place in the third century A.D. The Yamatai kingdom was located on the southern part of Japan and archeological findings affirm that Yamatai was located in Kyushu. The rulers of Yamatai, the Yamato, gained more power and established the imperial line which claimed to be the direct descendant of Amaterasu.

During the Yamato Period, the society was already classified in the ruling class, the Uji, and the serving class, the Be. These were specialized groups providing various services to the Uji class. The Yamato family itself was at first an Uji class and later turned into the imperial family. The entire Uji society was then ranked and classified by closeness to the imperial line.

These principles of social and political organization have provided Japan not only with a symbolic centrality and focus of identity but with the blueprint of social order that has been drawn on through the centuries which are still found in modern day Japanese society. During Yamato's reign, Japan was ruled according to the Chinese political structure, and for the first time the country was controlled by the civil and criminal law system. The Be system was dismissed and farmers became free tenants of the state and received a parcel of land for their own use (Hendry, 2004).

The city of Nara was built as the capital city of Japan, and a hundred years later, Heiankyo, the contemporary Kyoto, became the new capital city of Japan. That is why in Japanese history they speak about the Nara Period (A.D. 710–94) and the Heian Period (A.D. 794–1191). The imperial family, the Yamatos, ruled both periods.

From the time of the Yamatos establishing date, A.D. 300 until the end of Heian Period A.D. 1191, Japan was strongly influenced by the Chinese culture. Arts and culture bloomed and during the first five hundred years, poetry and literature flourished. Also architecture, Buddhist temples, and buildings were built.

This high period of Chinese influence in Japan was also marked by the acceptance of Buddhism both as a dominant religion and a powerful establishment. This religion was assured of the favor of the central Yamato nobility. Therefore, splendid temples were created at the expense of the government which was followed by rich Buddhist ceremonies. Buddhism as a religion and as a cultural force became an integral part of the aristocratic life (Hall, 1991).

Gradually, the imperial family lost its political power to the Fujiwara family. Due to the arranged marriage alliances, the Fujiwara's gained more influence and more Fujiwara rulers and chancellors and a few influential families ruled the country. These influential families gradually gained control over areas of cultivated land, and the direct relationship between the farmers and the government was replaced with farmers — local superiors — who were connected with the influential families. This makes an end to the aristocratic age and the start of the gradual process of feudalism in Japan. The Chinese model of bureaucracy lost its significance and the ruling families and establishment were more concerned with military skills. They developed a code of ethics and rules which gave birth to the Samurai warriors. These codes and ethics are called Bushido — the way of Samurai! Due to civil unrest, a strong military headquarter was established and gradually gained more political power and influence.

At the end of the twelfth century, Yoritomo, a strong military leader became the head of the military force, the chief commander with the title of Shogun. Ever since, the power of Shogun grew until 1868 when the Shoguns and Shogunates held the power in their hands. The system that had been developed since the calling of the first Shogun caused Japan to be divided into autonomous provinces under the leadership of local Shoguns. In Japanese these local Shoguns are called Shugos and Jitos. The farmers who cultivated the land parcels were obligated to provide their superiors — those working for the local Shogun — with rice and other products. In exchange, the local Shogun would give protection to the farmers because farmers were often the victims of battles between landlords because of disputes over the land and area. Here comes, then, the role of the Samurais, which were employed by the local Shoguns.

They had to protect them and their properties and the farmers as well. The Samurais gained more power during the Tokugawa Period (1603–1867).

According to John Whitney Hall, the spread of the particular practices which identify with the feudal syndrome did not occur suddenly or uniformly throughout Japan nor was it a sudden "break" with the imperial system. The encroachment of feudal practices, as identified with the ascension of the Samurai into political and economic leadership, came slowly over the course of many centuries. Historians have customarily divided this period into three: the Kamakura Period (1185–1333) when military leadership and feudal practice existed alongside with those of Kyoto courts; the Ashikaga or Muromachi Period (1338–1573) during which the

Samurais took over the remnants of the imperial system of government and eliminated most of the court proprietorships; and the Tokugawa Period (1603–1867) when the Samurai class stood unchallenged as the countries rulers relied increasingly on non-feudal means of government (Hall, 1991).

Japan Encounters Europe

During the Ashikaga Period in 1543, Japan encountered Europe with a shipwreck of three Portuguese sailors on the island of Tanegashima off the coast of Kyushu. This was the first encounter of two totally different cultures — the Japanese and the Europeans. This encounter had crucial consequences for Japan. The first was the introduction of firearms and the other was the introduction of Catholicism through the arrival of the Portuguese Jesuit priest, Francis Xavier. Later, I will be discussing the development of Catholicism in Japan and the hostility of the Japanese rulers towards this newly introduced faith.

TOKUGAWA OR EDO PERIOD (1603–1868)

The Tokugawa Period is one of the more interesting periods in Japanese history. By the end of the 1500s Japan was a decentralized nation ruled by military overlords and peasant confederations. At the end of the sixteenth century, Tokugawa Ieyasu, one of the small groups of warriors, put an end to this decentralized Japan. The battle of Sekigahara in 1600 and the victory of Tokugawa Ieyasu was the starting point of the Tokugawa Period, a period which lasted nearly three hundred years. After the battle of Sekigahara, Tokugawa established the foundation for an orderly and disciplinary government. Tokugawa and his descendants were able to centralize Japan under the leadership of the Shogun. During these 250 years of discipline, Japanese society was classified in various ranks and every one was forced into a certain social stratification and place.

The teachings of Confucius were the standard of living and belief alongside the religion of Buddhism in Japan. It was during the Tokugawa Period that certain Buddhist and Confucian rules became the main social and cultural ethic of the Japanese people. These will be discussed in more detail in the next chapter.

The Japan of the Tokugawa Period was an agricultural society and the economy depended on that. During this period Japan had approximately thirty million inhabitants. The Japanese population stagnated in the 1700s due to urbanization and the improved life standard, a gradually consumption-oriented lifestyle, and urban life activities of arts. Later on there came a shortage of food and this led to various famine disasters because of old fashioned agricultural methods and a relatively rapid population growth. The farmers' tax increased and due to a long peace period starting in 1620, the Samurai class gradually (at the end of this period) lost its military power but still maintained its symbolic stature. Some Samurais chose to become farmers and some worked as administrators. During this period, the emperor still existed but he had almost zero power; the country was simply ruled by local Shoguns, Shugos and Jitos.

In the Tokugawa Period, the War Lords or the Daimyo ruled the territories. Generally, there were three types of Daimyo: collateral Daimyo (shinpan), hereditary Daimyo (fudai), and outer Daimyo (tozama). In total there were somewhere between 254 and 295 Daimyo. Those in the first group were relatives or descendants of the first Tokugawa Shogun, Ieyasu Tokugawa. The second group was quite close to the Shogun and the last group, the Tozama, was never offered any central position or office during the Tokugawa Period (Lande, 1989).

The encounter with the West and the introduction of Catholicism did not impress the Tokugawa of Japan, and so they considered Europeans and their religion as a threat. Therefore, they chose an isolation policy, and for three hundred years Japan's doors were closed to Westerners with the exception of the Dutch. Why should Japan keep ties with the Dutch and not with the Portuguese and the Spaniards?

We have to realize that by the end of the sixteenth century and the beginning of the seventeenth century Japan was somehow open to foreign powers. The encounter with the Portuguese and the Spanish, plus some trade with South Asian countries like the Philippines and India, made Japan aware of the developments of the Spanish and Portuguese colonial ambitions in the region. The political ambition of these Latino European nations was parallel to their religious ambition, which was the spread of Catholicism throughout the world and also in Japan. This was directed by another religious-political power established in Rome — the Vatican.

The Dutch, however, were just emerging as a colonial nation and were the enemy of Spain because the Dutch were under the oppression of the Spaniards for many years. From the other side, the Dutch ambition to explore the sea was political and economical. The Dutch were more interested in trade and commerce which was less threatening to the Japanese. Relatively, the Dutch did not have a religious agenda with Japan because the Dutch did not have Rome behind them.

Society and Culture during the Tokugawa Period

The society was categorized in various classes: the Samurais, the military class, and the common population which was divided into three classes — the farmers, the artisans and the merchants. The merchants and the artisans were living in the cities and the farmers were in the rural areas.

The Tokugawa family ruled the nation for 250 years with absolute force. There were at the beginning 60,000 Samurai, and in the middle of this period there were about 300,000 Samurai of various ranks, skills, and occupations. The Samurai were professional military people who worked in the army and in the bureaucratic machine of the Tokugawa regime.

The strict Confucianism and Samurai ethics alongside the Buddhist religion helped the society to maintain this classification. Buddhism became the national religion in order to ban Christianity. Everybody had to become a registered Buddhist or else be killed.

During this period many Christians were martyred for their faith. In Chapter Seven I will be discussing this in more detail.

The Samurai ethics, or the way of the warrior, bushido, affected many in the society. Bushido emphasizes the ideal of selfless service to one's lord to be demonstrated by ostentatious self-denial, no drinking, no gambling, no extravagance, no over-eating, and no visits to the playhouse or brothel

(Bowring & Kornicki, 1993). During the Tokugawa Period, the emperor resided in Kyoto, whereby the Shoguns capital city was Edo, the contemporary Tokyo. The Shogun, Ieyasu, chose Edo, which back then was a small fishing community, to become his capital seat of government. He began to transform this town into a strong and appropriate city. He started building programs, draining systems, and marshlands. He constructed a great fortress surrounded by a network of canals and he attracted merchants and craftsmen with offers of free land and tax concessions. Within a century, the Shogun's capital had developed into one of the largest cities in the world with over a million residents. Half of these belonged to the Samurai class and the other half were people who provided services for the entire city population — carpenters, porters, fishmongers, greengrocers, tea sellers, cake makers, medicine makers, fabric makers, etc. (Bowring & Kornicki, 1993).

Also, the emperor's capital had, in the seventeenth century, a population of 600,000 people, and Osaka was also a merchandized city due to her sake and oil production. As we can see, the urbanization in Japan took place in seventeenth century, not due to the industrial revolution as we know in Europe, but due to the ambitious building and art projects of the Tokugawa Shoguns starting with Ieyasu, the first Shogun. There are historical documents which indicate the attempt of the government at that time to restrict urbanization and encourage the immigrants to go back to their rural areas.

During this period, the cities grew, and due to merchants and commerce, they became richer and richer. This gave birth to a new group — the merchant leaders. These leaders had economic powers and groups like retailers, bankers, investors, and shipping and transport business people, etc. Due to the rapid urbanization and the growth of commerce and arts literacy became essential in Japan. All over Japan in the villages and in the cities there were local temples where children would go to learn reading and writing. And at the end of this period, in some daimyo, there were schools established to teach literacy. This caused the literacy rate of Japan during that period to be around thirty-five percent, which was higher than other contemporary nations.

The relatively high literacy rate caused the emergence of the printing industry and the commercial printing of books, literature, and poetry. There were professional publishing companies publishing various types of literature like, stories, comic books, guide books, novels, religious literature, and also pornography.

The printing industry urged the Japanese to hunger for knowledge and this led to exploration in science and technology. The Dutch were also helpful in the new style of medicine, the European style.

The Impersonalization of the Japanese Citizens

All these political and social developments led to a changing position of the person as an individual; the society crystallized into various status groups, vertical and horizontal units, based on administrative bureaucratic levels. We may call this "impersonalization."

Confucianism played an important role in this process. Confucian thinking was based on a simple premise that there is a natural separation of society for status and occupation, and this thinking concentrated on absolute loyalty to your superior. This was then used by the Tokugawa regime in order to rule or govern the nation.

Another ideal aspect of Confucianism was that no one should abuse his position. Rulers should fulfill their duties as honest as possible, regardless of rank and status, including the government and administration system. However, this was just the ideal description and did not happen in reality. Based on this, Confucianism had made certain rules of fulfilling one's duty based on a specific class or status. Every person belongs to a certain class or status and has his/her own specific duties.

All duties begin with the family and the role of status within the family. The father has the highest status. Based on this, Confucianism created various 'duty-rules and regulations' between a man and a woman.

These kinds of 'duty-oriented regulations' were specifically made for every institution or class from family to government. During the Tokugawa Period, the Japanese people were forced to learn placing themselves in social classes and to do what was required of them. For 250 years the Tokugawa regime tried to impose these kinds of rules and regulations upon the Japanese people.

Bridge to Modernization

The Tokugawa Period is also recognized as the transitional period of Japan toward modernization and industrialization. In his article 'the Tokugawa period and Japan's preparation for modern economic growth' in the Journal of Japanese Studies, Sydney Crawcour writes that the roots of Japanese modernization have to be found in the Tokugawa Period. According to Crawcour, during the last fifty years of the Tokugawa Period the developments have been fast: the traditional loan system changed into a modern loan system, and the traditional agriculture turned into a commercial one. And the rural industries grew day by day. New commercial networks were created, and during the closing years of this period there were certain industrial factories in western style (Crawcour, 1974). At the end of this period dissatisfaction of the population grew day by day, and many blamed the Shogun for all of this. Also, the Buddhist priests were the cause of dissatisfaction, corruption, and moral decay among the people and the population distrusted them. Therefore, there was apathy towards Buddhism.

Since the emperor had no political role during this period, the Japanese people began to long for the emperor because Shinto, the Japanese traditional faith, is an emperor-adoring religion. In reaction to that the Shinto religion began to revive again.

Gradually Shogun was no more popular and eventually in 1867, the Shogun resigned from his power and the Tokugawa Period officially ended. In 1867, the new emperor came to power and ruled Japan until 1912. This period is called the Meiji Period, the period of the modernization of Japan.

MEIJI PERIOD (1868–1912)

The Meiji Period began with an ambitious program aiming to transform Japan into a modern, centralized national state in the West-European model — a nation with a strong military and economic power that was even better and more advanced than European states.

The Meiji Period is characterized by Bunmei-Kaika, meaning civilization and enlightenment, and followed by its two other important slogans: Fukoku Kyohei, a rich nation with strong army, and Oitsuki Oikose, catch up and pass — which means catch up with the West and pass them by — be better than they. There arose intellectual groups who saw the West offering civilization, science, and technology. One of these intellectuals was Fukuzawa Yukichi. He wrote several books on the subject of the western culture. Outline of Civilization, Conditions in the Western World and Encouragements of Learning are two of his important works.

Fukuzawa traveled to the West and he described in his books, especially in Conditions in the Western World, the West with her buildings, institutions, factories, streets, technology, etc. These things caught the attention of the people. Also, he believed in education as the foundation of modernity. Fukuzawa, himself, is the founder of one of the great universities today — Keio University. However, people like Fukuzawa did accept the Western civilization, yet they strongly believed in maintaining Japanese culture and religion. There were others who did not think that way. They believed that the western model without Christianity and the values of the Christian faith were empty, and Japan's modernization should go parallel with accepting and adopting the Christian faith in Japan. Namakura Masano was one of these thinkers. However, his ideas were not strongly accepted by others.

Soon a group of intellectuals was formed to begin the reformation in Japan. The central figures within the newly formed government were from various circles of the society who strongly fought for the restoration of the emperor's legitimate power and influence in national politics. These men were influenced by the writings and teachings of Fukuzawa and other scholars.

In total, there were nine leaders. Five were from the Samurai class. These leaders were called Genro, which means "the elders." These elders all agreed that Japan was a weak underdeveloped nation, and the only way for Japan to survive was to carefully maintain her in the midst of aggressive imperialistic nations. The first thing the elders did was to implement a ground tax which was provided during the first ten years of Meiji Period. It brought eighty to ninety percent of Japan's income.

The ground tax meant that the peasants, in place of paying a part of the harvest as they did in the Tokugawa Period, now had to pay money for every piece of parcel they cultivated. Due to this, many poor peasants could not afford the newly implemented system, and so many collapsed or began to work for bigger landowners. This was the beginning of rural capitalism because smaller peasants had no choice to survive and so they worked for bigger sized peasants instead. This also meant that the peasants had to produce for market and money.

Japan began to change drastically. The law system changed. People were considered "equal" according to the new law and the old crystallized classes were no longer valid. This, however, did not mean that the Japanese people had abandoned the 250 years long class system. They continued practicing it. They could not shift to the new system instantly. The political atmosphere changed during the 1870s when the first political parties were born.

In 1889, a constitution was promulgated which made provision for a bicameral parliament with an elected House of Representatives and an aristocratic House of Peers and a new legal system based on the French and German models (Hendry, 2004).

Foreign relations were improved and the isolationism of Japan began to end. However, the process began already at the end of the Tokugawa Period when the Tokugawa regime hired the Dutch, French, and the British to teach and train the army and teach foreign languages. This continued in the Meiji Period. Foreigners were hired to help Japan with her modernization. The British assisted the Japanese in establishing the railways, telegraph system, and lighthouses. Also, they helped Japan to modernize its navy. The French and Germans helped to modernize the land forces (Bowring & Kornicki, 1993).

However, the Japanese made an important decision, and that was to catch up with the West and pass western technology with the help of Japanese culture, especially the Japanese Confucian ethics and Shinto and Buddhist identities. This meant western technology, science, education and dress code. It also involved the Japanese ethics and spirit, the Samurai sense of loyalty and honor, etc. With this in mind, Meiji-Japan began her industrialization. They wanted to be far better and advanced than the West. Therefore, Japanese nationalism began to bloom. All of the people had one thing in mind and that was to transform Japan into a superpower. This is an interesting characteristic of Japan. History shows that Japan imported many things culturally, politically, and technologically from China or Korea and now from the West. Japan has no problem making her own that which was originally imported. I call this "Japanization process" — import and give a Japanese identity to it and then improve it and even export it back to where the original idea came from. This was true also after World War II with many different industries such as cars and electronics. First, Japan learned to imitate and make cheap cars. Later an improved Japanese version of the cars was ready for export!

As we may all know, it was Philips, a Dutch electronic company, that invented the CD player for the first time. Later Japan took this concept and even advanced the technology far better than the Dutch did themselves.

Industrialization

The industrialization of Japan was strongly linked to making Japan a strong military nation. Therefore, there was a need for specific industries that could provide services, goods, and techniques to the modern military demands of Japan. Iron industry for railways and for western style shipbuilding projects is one example. Therefore, the mining industry became more essential. Also, the communication industry emerged and telegraph lines were established in order to ease the administrative control and connection between various administrations. The textile industry began to flourish and there was a need for western style military uniforms since Japan aimed to modernize its army. The cotton and woolen textile industries rapidly grew.

Despite the modernization and industrialization, there was an economic crisis between 1877 and 1880. The high inflation caused devaluation of the land tax that government finances depended upon. Therefore, the government decided to privatize some non-strategic industries. However, Tokyo had difficulties with finding buyers for these industries. The government offered these industries for very cheap prices to people who were connected to the government or even government officials themselves. A few years later this gave profit to the newly privatized industries and the few who had been privileged to purchase these enterprises grew wealthy and came to control a large share of Japan's modernized economy. All these eventually contributed to the concentration of much of Japanese industry in the hands of a few giant corporations — the Zaibatsu (Reischauer & Craig, 1989). Mistui, Mitsubishi, Sumitomo and Yasuda are important Zaibatsu from this period.

Even today, Zaibatsu have control over many aspects of industry and commerce, from banking to shipping, construction and various industries. Mitsubishi, for instance, is one of the Zaibatsu. Mitsubishi is not only in the machinery or car business, but they are also in banking and other services.

Political Ambitions during the Meiji Period

Japan's growing nationalism and political ambitions during this period caused Japan to have problematic relationships with other Asian nations, especially its neighboring nation, China. As Japan grew stronger, friction between Japan and China increased with each seeking to dominate the Korean Peninsula. In 1882 they both stationed troops there (Bowring & Kornicki, 1993).

This caused the Sino-Japanese War in 1894 and 1895. Japan won this war. In this battle, Japan attacked Korea, and through Korea she entered China. Shocked, the western nations had no choice but to recognize Japan as a strong Asian military power. As result of a peace treaty, Japan received Taiwan as a territorial concession. This was the beginning of Japanese imperialistic attempts and ambitions. In 1905, Japan won another battle, this time from Russia, a western nation. This also surprised the world. During the First World War, Japan was allied with England and fought alongside the allied forces against Germany. Undoubtedly, Japan was now seen as one of the emerging world powers at that point of history.

Religion

During the Meiji Period, Confucian ethics, plus Shinto and Buddhism, were merged and became the national religions of Japan. In contrary to the Tokugawa Period, during the Meiji Period, Christians were relatively free. Christians played an important role in the formation of schools and universities. Christians also influenced the women's rights movement.

JAPAN DURING AND AFTER WORLD WAR II

The attack on Pearl Harbor in 1941 was the starting point of Japan's Pacific War against the allied forces which ended with the total surrender of Japan in 1945. The Japanese superpower ambitions and imperialistic adventures cost millions of lives in Asia and the Pacific islands. At the end, many Japanese people became victims themselves through the dropping of the atomic bombs on Hiroshima and Nagasaki. The Japan of 1945 was an occupied Japan, a conquered superpower, and a fallen imperialistic nation. What remained were the ruins of war, chaos, poverty, and disease. Japan, in the summer of 1945, was a nation exhausted both physically and morally says the historian and writer, John Whitney Hall, in his book, Japan. According to Hall, since the outbreak of the China war, 3.1 million Japanese, of whom 800,000 were civilians, lost their lives.

Over thirty percent of the Japanese lost their homes. There was a food shortage and the transportation system barely functioned. Acute food shortages brought much of the country to near starvation. Civilian morality broke down as farmers reaped tremendous profits by selling food on the black market. Wealthy families bartered heirlooms for the necessities of life. The industry had been smashed to one quarter of its previous potential capacity and the country was on the verge of inflation. The people also were emotionally and intellectually bewildered, having been brought up on exaggerated wartime propaganda and hyper-nationalist values, all of which collapsed with Japan's unconditional surrender (Hall, 1991).

Japan fell under the supervision of the Supreme Commander of Allied Powers, SCAP, under the leadership of general, Douglas MacArthur. According to the SCAP's policy, Japan had to go through three important phases: demilitarization, democratization, and rehabilitation.

Japan was totally dismantled. Certain laws which were imposed in the Meiji Period were no longer valid. Also, recognition of the deity of the Japanese emperor was abolished. Democratic laws were imposed and political parties played an important role on the political scene. Japan would be economically revived. The Korean War in the 1950s was an economic boost for Japan who provided a range of goods and services to U.S. forces in Korea.

Slowly, life began to normalize and the Japanese people began to believe in themselves again. In the early 50s and 60s, new technologies arose to revive some industries that were damaged during the war like the shipbuilding industry. Later, electronic devices like radios and other gadgets came onto the international economic scene. The automobile industry began to flourish. Later on the computer industry began to bloom. The society began to change. Western lifestyles with some basic Japanese values were continually on the run.

These values were adopted into Japanese company managements, and salary men, as the Japanese say, Salarymen, the working class in private and public sector, began to be an important group in Japanese society. For many years Japan had a low rate of unemployment and a low rate of crime. Yet these figures have been changing recently.

Once again, Japan turned out to be a superpower in the world. However, the society is beginning to change. Unhappy youth and a monotonous modern society are causing new social dilemmas. High rates of suicide and other types of maladies are appearing more and more in Japan. The Japanese game industry and the Internet have caused many to live an isolated life, especially the youth. Also, Japan became a pioneer of pornographic movies and magazines and an exporter of such videos and DVDs to other nations. Dirty sites combined with advanced Internet and computer technology were depraving the values of the Japanese society. These are some side effects of overdoses of 'modernity.'

Part Two
JAPANESE SOCIETY

INTRODUCTION

In the previous chapters, I briefly described the important episodes of Japanese history, especially the Tokugawa and Meiji periods because modern Japanese society is strongly rooted in the developments that took place during these two important periods. Many books have been written concerning the Japanese society and culture that help us better understand this nation.

Often, Japan is described as a harmonious mixture of traditional and modern societies where the traditional Japanese values are smoothly integrated within the modern westernized lifestyle. How smooth this integration has been is the issue at hand for many scholars and also a point of disagreement!

One of the classical writings on Japan is unavoidably, the Chrysanthemum and the Sword, by Ruth Benedict (1887–1948). Benedict was a professor of anthropology at Columbia University and a well-known American anthropologist. In 1944, she was assigned to study Japan and she used all the techniques she could use to spell out what the Japanese were really like (Benedict, 1989). Eventually, the American government and the army wanted to use her information to better know their enemy and use the information in their decision-making and war policy. In her book, Ruth Benedict described the Japanese culture as a culture with dualistic contradictions as the title of her book indicates. The Chrysanthemum and the Sword are two different things. Chrysanthemum is the Japanese flower, the symbol of Japanese beauty and how the Japanese adore beautiful things such the Chrysanthemum.

From the other side, the sword indicates the rudeness and harshness of this culture. In Part Four, I will deal with the Japanese culture in detail.

After Ruth Benedict, there have been many other scholars and writers who have dealt with Japan. Chie Nakane, of the 1970s, is another interesting sociologist and writer who published the book Japanese Society. In this book Chie Nakane gives a sociological and behavioral analysis of Japanese society.

During the late 1980s and 1990, the harmony theories of Japan began to be questioned and modern sociologists and other scholars began to proclaim that Japanese society is not a monotonous or harmonious society. Perhaps it was before, but now it has changed. In this part, I will be looking at basic understandings of the social aspects which shape the Japanese society and individual behavior in this nation. Glimpses of Japan's family life, social structures such as gender relations, work life, and education will be described.

CHAPTER 3

THE JAPANESE FAMILY

Understanding the Japanese family and even the Japanese society requires knowledge of the traditional Japanese family system which is called ie.

According to Reischauer, the pre-modern Japanese family, known as ie, might include a subordinate branch of families under the authority of the main family and other members who were distant kin or not related at all. It also gave absolute authority over the individual members to the father or the family council. This sort of family was to be found particularly among the more prominent members of the feudal warrior class, rich merchants, and certain peasant groups (Reischauer, 1988).

Ie is the indigenous term for family; however, it does not cover the exact meaning of the word "family" as we know in the West. Ie may be translated as 'house' or 'building,' but it is used in a broader way such as 'family' or 'kin.' It was a whole structure consisting of a main family and under that main family were various subfamilies.

In her book, Understanding the Japanese Society, Joy Hendry writes that continuity is a very important feature of the ie. The individual members of a particular house, who need not always be resident, occupy the roles of the living members of that particular ie. The total membership includes all those who went before: the ancestors, now forgotten as individuals, the recently dead who are remembered, and the descendants as yet unborn (Hendry, 2004).

In the traditional Japanese house we may find a Buddhist altar called Butsudan where the members remember their ancestors (senzo) and recently deceased individuals in the ie. Butsudan played an important role in the house especially when the family members were about to make important decisions or discuss important matters. They keep the door of Butsudan open so that the ancestors may listen and participate in the matters of the family.

Ie was a hierarchically oriented family system based on Confucian principles of honor and loyalty. This Confucian principle covered all the forms of relationships within the ie. Old-young relationships were based on loyalty and indebtedness, and relationships were duty oriented. Duty towards the members within the ie system was considered more important than anything else.

This duty-oriented system influenced the relations of men and women whereby men were considered much higher than women. Women were required to provide for every need of their husbands. Therefore, in the ie system, marriages were arranged according to social status and suitability in order to fulfill the woman's duty toward the ie of her husband. Love between husband and wife was not considered as essential, and it should not be a hindrance to the duty of a couple towards each other and towards the ie system.

After the surrender of Japan and the victory of the allied forces in 1945, the new established government abolished the ie family system. According to the new constitution, the family was defined as a nuclear unit and not a corporation of various family units. Due to the new constitution, women were treated equally with men and they had the same rights as men.

The abolishing of the ie system, however, does not mean that this system is totally dismissed in the society. For centuries Japan practiced this family system. Though in the law this system does not exist the influence of ie is visible in various aspects of society, for example in business corporations. I believe that zaibastu business culture is strongly based on the ie system. There are also some other aspects such as relationships which are still influenced by ie system. For example, even though women are free according to the law in some aspects women are still treated worse than men.

CONTEMPORARY JAPANESE FAMILY

The contemporary Japanese family looks like the traditional western style family with a father, mother, and children settled in urban areas living in little apartments. The mother cares for the children and the father works in a company or governmental institution or is running his own business.

How does an average modern age Japanese family function? It all begins at home. Japanese people have a very particular concept of home called uchi, which literary means "house" but also means "inside." Everything outside the house means soto, which literary means "outside." Uchi-Soto, however, does not only refer to the literal meaning of house, or inside and outside, but is a form of the ie family system.

In this case uchi means house and every thing that is related to inside inner territories. At the same time it may be related to clean, beautiful, and everything associated with good. Uchi may also be related to ie where someone belongs.

In contrary, soto means outside, outer territories, but it is also related to dirt, unclean, etc. That is why when the Japanese enter their homes, uchi, they take off their shoes so that they will not bring the dirt of the outside soto in their homes. In another part of this book, I will be discussing the Uchi-Soto system in a cultural framework.

Children

Let us analyze the Japanese family by starting with the children. Children in their early ages are trained to become aware of hierarchy and to find their place at home and outside. Children are trained to think and act in the group they belong to and then to move individually. They are trained from a very early age to think of the good of others and to do to others as they would want others to do to them. Japanese kids are raised up to be group-oriented and not self-oriented. Consequently, every group may belong in various settings and times that make that group to be their uchi. One has to act for the sake and good will of the uchi where they belong. It can be at home with other siblings or at kindergarten or as classmates.

The personalized collective term mina-san is used to address and refer to the whole group and its needs. An individual whose behavior is to the detriment of mina-san is made to feel most uncomfortable (Hendry, 2004). There is a saying in Japanese, deru kugi wa utareru, meaning "the nail which sticks up, will be pounded down." This proverb is a very good example of how the children are being trained from the early age of the formation of their character.

Also, at schools they are trained not to say much and not to ask many questions because it may disturb the group and that may be considered a selfish act.

In the nuclear families, it was common for the wife to stay at home and raise the children and be involved in the matters of the house, uchi. In contemporary Japan, this is gradually changing. More than fifty percent of married women are working. Parents are too busy to take care of their children. Therefore, the number of children is decreasing. In early postwar Japan, the husbands worked and the wives took care of their children. This is disappearing and children are hardly loved by their parents. The children have to spend a lot of time alone. With the coming of computers and the Internet things have become worse. The children communicate with the computer and Internet while contact with the outside world becomes poorer and weaker. This means that many of them have or will have many mental problems.

On Sunday, October 20, 2002, BBC World News reported the following: "Teenage boys in Japan's cities are turning into modern hermits — never leaving their rooms: Hikikomori! Pressure from schools and an inability to talk to their families are suggested causes" (BBC News, 2002).

Hikikomori are adolescents and young adults who feel overwhelmed by the Japanese society. They feel unable to fulfill their expected social roles and react with social withdrawal. Hikikomori often refuse to leave their parent's houses and may lock themselves in a single room for months or even years.

According to some estimates, there may be one million hikikomori in Japan, or 1 out of 10 young men. Most of them are male and many of them are the eldest sons.

There is a lot of pressure on adolescents and young adults in Japan. The immediate society expects them to be "successful." The pressure comes from a number of different sources. One of the biggest concerns for Japanese adolescents is their performance in the educational system where they often face significant pressure from parents and the society in general. In extreme cases the pressure starts already before pre-school where they have to pass an entrance exam to get into the best pre-school. This prepares the children for the entrance exam for the best kindergarten which in turn prepares the child for the entrance exam for the best primary school, junior high school, high school, and eventually university. Another source of pressure is from their co-students who may harass and bully some students for a variety of reasons including physical reasons. This is especially true if the student is overweight or has a perceived weakness in intelligence, athletics, wealth, or ethnicity. Some have been punished for bullying and truancy which brings shame to their families (hikikomory in www.answers.com).

Wives, Mothers, and Women

The majority of marriages in Japan are arranged marriages, miai. Many of the women enter into a marriage by the arrangement of others. However, it is difficult to judge how many marriages are established based on affections.

Most contemporary couples describe their marriages as "in-between" which means that someone introduced them and then they fell in love and decided to marry. Love alone is still not viewed as a sufficiently solid basis for marriage. The young Japanese couple is more cognizant than its American counterparts for the need for social support to keep the marriage going. Family investigations are an important precursor for marriage decisions, and a Japanese man or woman is still unlikely to marry a partner who is opposed by the family (Imamura, 1990).

Once again we can see that even within the modernity of Japanese society tradition still plays an important role, and some elements of the traditional ie system are still valid. This will raise the question, "What is love and what is the border between love and matrimonial duties? Do the couples feel love for one another or do they have to pretend? Or do the Japanese have a different understanding of love?"

In nuclear families, especially those of men who work for big companies, it has become common for a woman to stay at home, keep the house, and attend to the small children. She is usually entrusted with the family finances as well. Some women take this role so seriously that they are called "professional housewives." They have considerable input concerning their children's education, diet, and well being in general. However, more than fifty percent of the married women actually go out to work, and many others help in a family business or take piecework into the home (Hendry, 2004).

The duties of the wife do not end up in caring for the household, the husband, and the children. The fact that the life expectancy of the Japanese people, and in particular the women, is the highest in the world makes life harder for wives because they have to care for the elderly in the family who now live longer than before and demand special attention and care. This responsibility, combined with childcare and housework, often conflicts with the responsibility of holding a full time job. Due to lack of sufficient aid for working parents and not enough daycare centers and preschools, and since the family life is not expected to interfere with the husband's work, mothers choose to leave their jobs for the sake of educating and raising their children. This makes for major burdens on the wife. However, recently many women are beginning to put off marriage and children in favor of their careers. There are two types of women. One does not want to marry and she stays single. The other gets married but chooses to have no kids. This leads to other social problems, namely the average marriage age has become higher than before, and the number of single households or childless households has grown more than ever.

The position of women in Japanese society is changing day by day. But at the workplace there exists discrimination against them. Most women earn less than their male counterparts, and it is quite difficult for women to get higher positions within a company or organization. Women have only 0.1 percent of the board member positions in Japan's top companies. At the same time, many female workers in Japan have gone through sexual harassment and verbal and physical abuse.

Unfortunately, there are not enough registered/reported cases of such harassment because people do not easily report abuses in order to avoid public court cases. They attempt to keep the face of the family up and keep the record of the family reputation intact. In a recent survey of female civil servants, seventy percent reported that they had been sexually abused at least once. However, in the past ten years, only about one hundred sexual harassment cases have been registered in Japan. This occurs rarely because the Japanese people feel culturally ashamed to report these kinds of sexual harassments for fear that they may lose face. Therefore, they choose to suffer in silence.

Fatherless Society

Postwar Japanese families are often referred to as "fatherless." Japanese fathers are not very involved with their children. Long work hours and after work fellowships with colleagues mean fathers are away from home most of the day. As a consequence, they are less available to have time with their wives and children.

The word "fatherless" describes two major situations. First it refers to those families where the father has less time to be with the family due to a hectic and busy work life. Those families of which the father is lacking due to divorce or separation describe the other situation. Both situations are alarming in Japan. A 1994 education ministry survey showed Japanese fathers spent an average of 3.32 minutes a day with their children on weekdays.

On average, the fathers have seventeen minutes per day with their children's care. This means quality time and caring time for the kids (Ishii-Kuntz, date unknown). In the second case, the real "fatherless" families, meaning no father at home at all, is increasing daily.

A Japanese government survey published in early 2005 estimated that the number of fatherless families has gone up tremendously up to 1.22 million families in fiscal year 2003. This is the highest number ever registered in the history of Japan. It indicates a 28.3 percent increase from the previous survey conducted in the year 2000. The figures also show that the vast majority of children in these households live far below the poverty line, creating a rapidly expanding underclass of impoverished families. Beginning in February 2005, a twenty-seven year old woman and her three year old son were found starved to death in their apartment in the Saitama prefecture near Tokyo. Police reported that there was no food in the apartment and the woman only had eight yen (0.07 US dollars) in her purse (Curtin, 2005).

The 28.3 percent increase in fatherless families is due to the growing divorce rate in Japan which is, in turn, due to the lifestyle. Fathers, too busy to be husbands and fathers, are key figures in the dissolution of a strong family fellowship. Lack of a strong paternal influence and responsibility in the home has many negative effects on society. It is apparent that workaholic fathers create fatherless homes which have generated a rash of teenage angst and occasionally shocking outbursts of violence.

Education experts here say: "Fathers who do not understand what it means to raise children and who do not cooperate in the process are causing anxiety among many children and mothers." This was a report by an advisory panel to the education minister. As the presence of fathers has been weakened at home, children are inclined to read their mother's faces and make efforts to be a "good" boy or girl to please their mothers. Meanwhile, children tend to picture their fathers more as a friend than as a parent, and they are not getting enough discipline from them about what is good and bad. A 1996 survey by the Japan Youth Research Institute on one thousand youths each in China, Japan and the United States, showed a relative absence of guilt among Japanese teenagers who performed acts widely considered as bad. As many as 84.7 percent of Japanese students said they had the "freedom" to rebel against their parents. This compares with 16.1 percent in the United States and 14.7 percent in China. It also showed that 9 percent of Japanese students thought it was okay to extort money from others. This compares with 8.1 percent among their U.S. counterparts and 1.6 percent among Chinese students. Prostitution was not a bad thing for 25.3 percent of Japanese students. For Chinese youth this is 2.5 percent (France-Presse, 1998).

However, these numbers are not indicating the overall picture concerning Japanese fathers. The majority of the fathers are hardworking people who within the framework of their job do make time to have fellowship and communication with their wives and children.

The Elderly

It is proper to end this chapter with the elderly. The Japanese society is getting older. The birth rate is going down and it is estimated that in 2040 one-third of the population will be over sixty-five years old and only eleven percent will be under the age of fourteen (Hendry, 2004). A growing number of elderly people are unable and unwilling to rely on family members to help them go through the final years of their lives (ibid).

Despite the romantic image of the elderly spending time with their families and grand children, in reality, many of them are spending their closing years isolated from the younger generation. One indication of the yearning for an ideal family complete with grandchildren is depicted in the demand for a paid service called "service of the heart." One company, which has provided such a "rent a family" service since 1990, reported a high demand for the service, so much so that they had to place many elderly couples or individuals on the waiting list for visits from their purchased "family members." A typical rent-a-family session simulates a three-generation family setting. The "daughter" or the "daughter-in-law" — a trained entertainer — would prepare meals where all would eat together. And there would also be other "family" events such as family walks in the park, gift giving, singing, and chatting and playing with "grandchildren" who usually climb on the "grandparents" laps for intimate games with them (Thang, 2002).

This sad but true story indicates that the Japanese society, especially the family, is not improving but rather is going in the wrong direction. This is caused by the lack of interaction between the family members where the real society begins.

CHAPTER

4

JAPANESE WORKING LIFE

The Japanese are known as hard working people. They work longer and they are almost never absent from their work. This is the image many have about the Japanese working force. In this chapter, I will be dealing with Japanese work life and working culture and how this may affect the society. In general, the Japanese employees are called salaryman, an adopted English word brought over into Japanese.

We have to realize that Japan is a group society. This means there is a huge emphasis on group and belonging to the group. As I mentioned in a previous chapter, the Japanese call this uchi meaning "house" but also "inside," which begins with the family. However, uchi does not end up in family alone; it can take various forms depending on the circumstances. In this case, the company or the place where people work becomes uchi and the colleagues become the members of the family.

The Japanese companies function quite differently from their European or American counterparts. This, however, has changed in recent years. Basically, Japan knows the lifetime employment system. This means the workers stay in one company their entire working lives. Based on this principle, a unique Japanese company culture and lifestyle was born. Normally, schools and universities have contracts with companies, and as soon as the students graduate, they may have a place in a certain company. For decades this was the case for the recruiting working force, and this was one of the reasons why Japan had a low percentage of unemployment.

This is why group activities, group arrangements of various services, and company benefits are important in Japan. Working in Japan does not only mean having a good skill in your job, but it also means fitting in with the culture of the company. As the Japanese say: "We must love our company."

In Japan it has always been believed that individual moral and mental attitudes have an important bearing on productive power. Loyalty towards the company has been highly regarded. A man may be an excellent technician, but if his way of thought and his moral attitudes do not accord with the company's ideal, the company does not hesitate to dismiss him. Men who move in from another company at a comparatively advanced stage in their working life tend to be difficult to mold or they are suspect in their loyalties (Nakane, 1970). Since this type of lifetime employment system is a family-like group, it also pervades the private lives of the employees. This is crucial for group unity because the foundation of the individual's total emotional participation in the group helps to build a closed world and results in group independence or isolation (ibid).

Companies also provide various services and benefits such as pensions, health care, and often accommodations to their employees. Dormitories for unmarried workers, apartments for families, and even larger houses for senior employees are also part of these kinds of benefits. There are also sports facilities and holiday resorts for the employees. In some companies, sexual activities for male employees are common. Some companies believe that sexual intercourse may release the workers from stress. Some companies who do not have the resources for hiring prostitutes to do such jobs have special rooms where the employees may watch pornographic movies in order to release their stress.

However, in return, the employees are expected to perform with maximum input. Also, they should take fewer holidays and their leisure time should be spent with colleagues drinking in the local bars, playing sports together, or going on office trips.

In the framework of a group-oriented system, there are peer level and senior/junior interactions on individual levels. In the majority of companies, the boss or the leader is considered as the father of the house. As such, he may intervene with private issues of his employees such as finding a spouse for his employees or playing the role of matchmaker. Another aspect of Japanese working life concerns the company you belong to. Japanese people do not ask what you do for a living. They want to know where you work. Work in Japan means belonging to a group which is your working family, especially when someone belongs to big companies or institutions. Each institution may have its own songs or anthems, and singing these songs makes the employees and employers feel a sense of unity.

There are also various religious rituals going on in the majority of big companies. For example, one very famous electronic company has a special sanctuary to worship gods and ancestors who became gods.

There are also statutes of famous Japanese and international scientists such as Thomas Edison whereby the employees pay a visit and worship. Thomas Edison is honored as the god of electricity. These kinds of rituals are rooted in Japanese culture and are still being practiced in many major companies.

During my research I discovered that Japanese companies have somehow created their own company religion with rites and ceremonies designed to bolster the work atmosphere and sense of unity. Therefore, the majority of Japanese companies do not want people who are a member of a religious society because they cannot afford their employees being loyal and committed to another institution. Thomas P. Rohlen did fieldwork study in a Japanese bank and studied the management and working culture of that particular company. In his book, "For Harmony and Strength," he described the particular ceremonies that took place. He talked about performing various catechisms during the ceremony of joining the company.

First, they sing the company anthem together. In his research he found out something interesting. The bank does not want to employ members of "new religions" that require considerable time and effort on the part of their members. This is not because these religions are considered bad; on contrary, the bank sees many of them as positive moral forces in Japanese life. But the bank does not want its members to divide their loyalties. Also, the religious behavior of the parents of the candidate employee is important. If they are religious zealots of some sort, then the bank is not interested in having their children (Rohlen, 1974).

Japanese companies have created their own religion and what they practice is not less than any other type of religious group. Not employing people from religious groups indicates the rivalry between "company-religion" and religion.

Performance Oriented System

Japan is not only made of big or major enterprises or institutions. The majority of the companies are medium or small-sized enterprises such as family businesses. These companies are, however, different. Of course, the loyalty towards the work and the group is still valid for the middle-sized or small-sized companies. These companies cannot provide the same benefits as the big companies.

This doesn't mean that familiarity is not strong in these companies. On the contrary, because of their smaller size, the group unity and input for the business is even stronger than the larger companies. The society in Japan is changing rapidly and this also affects the working life in Japan. In contemporary Japan, there is a growing shift from a lifetime work system to a performance oriented work system. A Ministry of Labor survey has confirmed that the income of college graduates aged 40–45 varied more widely in 1998 than in 1993.

Many say that the growing gap reflects the new preference for performance-based pay (Wojtan, 2000). A performance oriented working system means many employees will not be paid based on seniority and the length of time a person has been working in a certain company. But rather, it will be based on the performance and achievements of an employee.

Another tendency in Japanese working culture is for young people to work part time and have more than one job. This group of people is called, furii-taa, meaning "free person," people who are free and unwilling to assume the lifestyle of an average salaryman.

Whether it is the Japanese lifetime work system or performance system, both are not healthy for the society. The first one may give economic stability or a low rate of unemployment, but its working culture and group expectations affect the family. The fathers are often tired and have less time to spend with their families. And even some activities that are expected from the employees, such as prostitute visitations, may affect the husband-wife relationship. It may hurt the wives. Even if they do not say anything they are suffering on the inside. In place of being with the wife or kids, the employee often goes out with colleagues and the boss. They drink in bars, get drunk, and come home drunk. Or they sleep in the street drunk, and the next day they go to work again.

Even in England and America, brothers and sisters meet much more frequently than is required by Japanese standards. Christmas is one of the great occasions when these kinfolk gather together. New Year's Day is Japan's equivalent to Christmas for those who live in the West. Everyone is busy with preparations for visits from subordinate staff, and then in turn they call their superiors.

There is little time and scope to give to collateral kin such as married brothers, sisters, cousins, uncles and aunts and so on, though the parents and grandparents will certainly be visited if they do not live in the same house (Nakane, 1970).

When work, not family, becomes the center of life what do you expect from a society? It may soon be fatigued, frustrated, and suffering. Then you get the counterpart of a lifetime working system, the performance based system. This system may be worse than the first because the first one at least had a sense of group loyalty, respect, seniority, and equal distribution of income.

The performance-based system makes society compete even harder and do everything for money and increase. This performance-based system makes the gap between poor and rich bigger. In reaction to both systems, there comes the furii-taa, the free man who does not fit and is not willing to fit into these systems.

These free men want to be free and too much of these freedoms may cause another social phenomena, "the parasite singles." These are singles between the ages of 20 and 35 who remain dependent on their parents.

They live with them, pay no rent, do no home work, or help with the house. What they do is to be furii-taa, working part time here and there, spending their money for expensive clothing, jewelry and shopping outside Japan, like going to Korea and other neighboring countries.

CHAPTER 5

SOCIAL STRATIFICATION IN JAPAN

When visiting Japan for business purposes, one will notice that when two people meet for the first time they immediately will exchange calling cards. This is a very important custom in Japan because by exchanging calling cards one's position will be clear and the other person will know where to place the other. Based on the information on the calling card a whole set of mannerisms and treatments will take place; language usage will be immediately adopted based on the position of the counterpart. The one with the lower rank will bow deeper than the one with the higher rank.

How do the Japanese conceptualize dimensions of social stratification? Japanese equivalents of class and stratum, kaikyu and kaiso, are both terms translated from English. The Japanese have a clear conception of stratification in their society even if their notions may be conceptually identical to their Western counterparts. One can easily list several Japanese terms describing the dimensions of stratification. Kaku denotes a finite series of ranks. As a generic term it can be applied by a wide range of ranking systems. Mibun implies a status position into which one is born. The term kakei, family line, has a similar connotation, which more explicitly emphasizes lineage and pedigree. In contrast, chii means a status position one achieves over time (Sugimoto, 2003).

Chie Nakane explains in her book, Japanese Society, that groups in Japan may be identified by applying two criteria: one is based on the individual's common attribute and the other on the situational position in a given frame. Frame may be a locality, an institution, or a particular relationship which binds a set of individuals into one group. In all cases it indicates a criterion which sets a boundary and gives a common basis to a set of individuals who are located or involved in it (Nakane, 1970). Attribute, however, means being a member of a definite group or caste. Attribute may be acquired not only by birth but also by achievement (ibid).

These criteria serve to identify the individuals in a certain group which can in turn be classified within the whole society even though the group may or may not have a particular function of its own as a collective body (ibid).

Within the framework of what I just described in this chapter, I will be dealing with certain important elements of social stratification in Japan. Just like many other societies, the basis of stratification is founded in gender, income, education, and ethnicity. Of course there are more. However, these that I have mentioned are more relevant for this research.

WOMEN AND GENDER INEQUALITY

In chapter three I have been describing the role of Japanese women within the family. In this chapter, however, I will be describing the role of women in the society and how the society views women and what are some problematic issues concerning gender equality in Japan. We have to realize that Japan is a very male-oriented society which finds its roots in the Confucian philosophy.

The Meiji restoration was a new start for Japanese women but it was not an improvement for the position of Japanese women. Women were taken into the industrialization and modernization process whereby they became a cheap working force. The transition from feudal society to industrial capitalist society brought forth various forms of illusions leading to riots, strikes, and all types of illness such as cholera. These illusions influenced the position of women and gave birth to various women's movements in Japan which began as strong opposition against the miserable position of women during the Meiji restoration.

The very first women's movements in Japan were influenced by basic elements of Christianity which were fighting legal prostitution in Japan. The Women's Temperance Association in Japan was a counterpart of the western organizations such as Women's Christian Temperance Union. One of the important movements in Japan, Jiyu Minken Undo or Movement for Freedom and Popular Rights, began in the 1880s. Kishida Toshiko (1864–1901) and Fukuda Hideko (1865–1927) were the central figures of this movement. Kishida's strong and charismatic speeches inspired many women in Japan; she fought for equal rights for women. Later on Fukuda joined Kishida and together they began the Popular Rights Movement.

Many other movements and various famous personalities continued to promote the feminist movement in Japan. People such as Yosano Akiko (1878–1942) or Hiratsuka Raisho and the socialist Yamakawa Kikue (1890–1980) should not be overlooked. Hiratsuka Raisho wrote the following poem:

> In the beginning, woman was the sun
> An authentic person
> Today, she is the moon
> Living through others
> Reflecting the brilliance of others...

The contemporary Japanese woman has many rights including equal rights to vote, education, and participation in the working sector. But still deep within the heart of the society, there are cultural biases and hidden ideas about women which are still rooted from the times of the Tokugawa and Meiji periods.

How about unmarried women, widows, and divorced women? How does society view them and treat them? For example, society views a divorced woman as strange, weak, and childish. Even if the man misbehaves the woman is blamed and made to feel ashamed (Meywis & Walle, 1989).

In Japan, for instance, there are no legal ways to force a divorced man to take care of his ex-wife financially. The law bans gender discrimination and proclaims equal rights for men and women, but these laws are only on paper and do not affect real life situations. Also, gender inequality is visible in educational attainment and the labor market. Inequality in gender does not exist at the high school level but it does at the university level.

This inequality, however, finds its roots in the family and how parents treat their children. For instance, Japanese parents pay eighty percent of their children's educational expenses. However, the parents invest in the university education of their son instead of their daughter because they can expect more advantages by doing so. In other words, the boys come first.

By writing this I do not mean that all Japanese parents are like this, but many are. Labor market studies show that the women's labor force participation is now more than fifty percent, but the majority of these women work in the secondary labor market and perform jobs that require little skill or training.

In companies, when a lady is getting more than twenty-four years old, she should look for a husband and build up her family and fulfill her duties as a wife. In some cases, the president or the boss of the company may approach the young lady advising her to build up her family and even help her find a proper husband. Gender inequality is somehow rooted culturally and, in the case of Japan, there are no exceptions.

INCOME AND UNEMPLOYMENT

Japan, which has long regarded itself as the most egalitarian industrialized nation, is seeing a widening gap between the rich and the poor that is spurred by extensive economic and social changes. Where once everyone was treated more or less the same, now due to factors such as longer life spans, women in the workforce, and pay based on performance rather then seniority, a stark contrast can be seen between the wealthy and the poor.

This increasing income stratification raises potentially troubling questions for Japan. Sameness or the perception of it greatly contributes to the social harmony that the Japanese people have historically prized. Government officials concede privately that greater income disparity is inevitable as the economy becomes more competitive. But they fear that differences between the rich and the poor will lead to more theft, petty crime, and a host of other social problems.

The disparities that exist between the classes in Japan, however, are far less pronounced than they are in the United States and Britain. An average chief executive in a large Japanese company makes roughly $350,000 (U.S. dollars) a year. An average worker's salary is around $56,000. By comparison, total compensation in 1998 for chief executives at the five hundred largest American companies was about $8 million (Storm, 2000).

Income inequality also depends on the level and the rank of job or the work a person is doing. Also, gender plays an important role in the inequality of income and assets in Japan.

Unemployment is another growing problem in Japan. In the 1960s, the golden period of Japanese economy, the unemployment rate remained in the range between 1.0 and 2.0 percent. In the 1970s after the first oil crisis in 1973, the unemployment rate went above two percent and almost three percent at the end of the 80s.

From 1990–91, there was an improvement but with the new millennium it increased again and reached five percent. However, in 2004 there was a slight change and the rate dropped below 5 percent to 4.6 percent.

In 2003, there were 3.5 million unemployed people. Of these people, 1.46 million were involuntarily dismissed because of payroll cutbacks, poor business conditions, mandatory retirement, and other reasons. Another 1.13 million voluntarily left their jobs for personal or family reasons. The number of new job seekers who just graduated from school was 200,000 while new job seekers for other reasons was 690,000.

Viewed in terms of age, the unemployment rate for both men and women in 2003 was highest among young people aged 15–19 (men, 13.3 percent; women, 10.5 percent) followed by men and women aged 20–24 (men, 11.2 percent; women, 8.2 percent).

These statistics reveal the high rate of unemployment among people in young age brackets. One of the reasons for the high unemployment rate among young people is that the number of young people who voluntarily quit their jobs is increasing. This is due to the difficulty that young graduates experience in finding satisfactory jobs in an extremely harsh employment environment where employment opportunities are quite limited. Unemployment among men aged 60–64 was 9.2 percent in 2003. Older workers who have been forced to leave their jobs before the normal retirement age as part of corporate restructuring programs are finding it extremely difficult to find the next job. Among those older than the retirement age of 60, there is a growing gap between the strong desire to work and the available employment opportunities. The same conditions apply to women aged 25–34 (6.8 percent) who are seeking to reenter the workforce (Ministry of Internal Affairs and Communications).

Being unemployed is not only a financial issue for a person, but it is also a health issue. For example, being unemployed leads to lower self esteem and a loss of attachment to the society. It can even stimulate crime and instability in the society.

EDUCATION

Japanese education has raised many questions among scholars and educators. Some praise it and some criticize it. Some believe that due to the strong emphasis on group and unity, the individual aspects of a child are ignored. From the other side, the strong authoritarian education system makes a child frustrated. Some suggest that this may even lead to suicide.

Once students have been accepted into a school, the Japanese very skillfully avoid overt competition among them and downplay differences in ability. In fact, almost no one fails. But the ruthless entrance examinations are competition at its worst and cast a shadow far in advance, subjecting the students to severe pressures throughout most of their schooling and distorting the content of their education. Much of the training in senior high schools is devoted not to learning as much but to preparing students to pass university entrance examinations (Reischauer, 1988).

From the other hand, some believe that this system is quite a unique system, teaching the children unity, harmony, and discipline; we call this moral education. In Japan, going to school does not only mean learning knowledge, but Japanese education emphasizes moral education such as diligence, endurance, deciding to do hard things, wholehearted dedication, and cooperation.

For example, children are clustered in work groups whereby they have to cooperate together to keep their school clean. Also, physical education is very important. School children have to exercise every morning.

The Japanese educational system is group oriented and the cohesion of the group is more important than individual competition in classes. Therefore, culturally, it is not polite for a student or a child to ask many questions from the teacher because he or she may disturb the group for his or her own personal interests. In sports, also, the group is emphasized over the individual.

How does the school where one studies and the university where one graduates affect the stratification in Japan? This is simple to explain. The school or university one graduates from determines the sort of job that person will have and in which company or institution that person will work. For instance, it is very prestigious to graduate from Tokyo University. The graduates from this university have more advantages. For instance, many state employees and high ranking politicians graduate from this university. Normally, companies have a relationship with schools and universities where they recruit their employees. Recruitment into these big businesses and government is done by examination. From the other side, many prestigious companies and government institutions invite only candidates from more prestigious universities and colleges to take recruitment examinations. This makes the pressure to enter prestigious universities much harder and stressful to the students, but this will determine the rank and the place these students will achieve within the Japanese society for their entire lives.

Here are some prestigious universities according to the ranks. Tokyo University is at the top. Next come Keio and Waseda universities. Then there are the national universities in each prefecture in Japan.

ETHNICITY: MINORITIES IN JAPAN

Japan has five major minority groups: Burakumin (a caste-based group); Okinawans (an indigenous group); Ainu (an indigenous group); Japanese-born Koreans; and migrant workers from other countries. Discrimination against many of these groups has its origins in the imperialist and feudal periods in Japan's history.

In the eighth century, the Japanese expanded their territory into the lands of the Ainu and Okinawans, two indigenous groups whose lands have now been annexed into modern day Japan.

Discrimination from Japan's feudal society also exists against the outcasts called the Buraku. Up to this point, there have been no Buraku and only one Ainu in the Diet, Japan's national parliament. For thirty-five years, Korea was under Japanese control. During World War II, Japanese soldiers forced many Korean women into sexual slavery. Migrant workers have arrived in Japan in search of a better life but instead have faced a great deal of discrimination from Japanese employers, the government, and Japanese nationals. Doka seisaku, a policy in which a nation endeavors to make the lifestyles and ideologies of the people in its colonies conform to its own, have affected many of these minority groups.

Japan has also followed a peculiar dual policy in regard to minority groups — forcing assimilation into the cultural mainstream on the one hand and developing measures to segregate them on the other (Human Rights Features, 2001).

Yoshio Sugimoto writes the following: "In every day life, racism and ethnocentrism still remain strong in many sections of the community and establishment" (Sugimoto, 2003). Japan's racial and ethnic homogeneity go hand in hand with Japan's belief that "Japaneseness" has superior qualities and should not be contaminated (ibid).

As I mentioned earlier, the Japanese population is getting older and the childbirth rate has dropped drastically. Therefore, Japan will be confronted with a very important issue. Do its people mix with other races or not? Will Japan survive this crisis?

In 1986, the Prime Minister, Yasuhiro Nakasone, publicly claimed that the Japanese people have a higher level of intelligence than Americans. This is because the Japanese race has remained pure. In 1990, Seiroku Kajiyama, the Minister of Justice, linked the influx of foreign prostitutes into a red-light district in Tokyo to the movements of blacks into white communities in the United States (ibid).

If prominent leaders in Japan think this way, how should an average Japanese person look at the outcasts and ethnic groups? Let us go through the five major groups in Japan and examine their life circumstances.

The Burakumin

The word Burakumin ("People of the Hamlet") refers to Japan's traditional "unclean" caste also known as Eta ("abundant pollution") and Hinin ("non-human"). During the Tokugawa Period, they were forced to live in separate villages and perform society's dirty jobs including grave digging, butchery, executions, and other low profile jobs. Almost two percent of the Japanese people are Buraku, and although they are racially identical to other Japanese people, discrimination is rampant. Caught in a vicious cycle of poverty and prejudice, many people are forced to invent "clean" family histories. The class was officially abolished in the Emancipation Act of 1871, but it is common for an employer to check an applicant's background for Buraku heritage. Protective parents often hire private detectives to make sure their child's potential spouse doesn't have any Buraku or Korean blood. Igarashi Terumi, a member of the Buraku caste, explains her experience as inhuman when she writes: "I was first told of my Buraku origins when I was seven years old, not by my parents, but by a non-Buraku child. At school other children taunted me with 'you are dirty!' 'You smell!' 'Don't come near me!' They tied my hands behind my back, put worms and snakes on me, and threw rocks at me when I tried to run away from their cruelty." Later on she grew up and with much difficulty she found a job. She said, "I took a job with a company where I continued to experience discrimination. My supervisors declared that I was poorly educated and had no ability. My colleagues would talk behind me saying, 'Her blood is different.' 'She eats different food!' 'She is a fool!' "They have eye diseases!" Unable to handle such treatment, I moved from job to job" (Francis & Nakajima, 1991). These are some interesting statistics about the Burakumin: almost eight percent of the Burakumin live in a minimum income situation to survive. Twelve percent live under the minimum tax standard income, and ninety percent of all Burakumin have an income lower than the average national income (Meyvis & Walle, 1989).

Ainu People and Okinawans

The Ainu people are the aborigines of northern Japan. For more than ten centuries these people have been discriminated against by Japan's central government attempting to annex their territories. During the history they have been considered as savages. They have lost their original language. Still, the Japanese government has not recognized the Ainu as indigenous people of Japan or given them the level of financial and moral support that indigenous people receive in other industrialized societies (Sugimoto, 2003).

The case of the Okinawa people is somehow similar to the Ainu people. Okinawa is the southernmost prefecture of Japan and the main island of the Ryukyu island chain. Because Okinawa had been the half-independent Ryukyu Kingdom until 1879, Okinawa has a culture and a language that are different from mainland Japanese.

Many Japanese people consider the Okinawans as foreigners and outsiders. This makes it difficult for the Okinawa people to find jobs in the mainland, and they are coming up short with other opportunities in life.

The Koreans

There are approximately 600,000 North and South Koreans in Japan today. The majority of them were born and grew up in Japan. A majority of them are the third and even the fourth generation were brought up here. Yet, the Japanese nationality is based on lineage, meaning that these Korean descendants are not automatically awarded Japanese citizenship. This is very hard to understand from a western point of view. A third or fourth generation African in Europe or America is automatically a citizen and obtains nationality. This is not the case in Japan. Once a Korean forever a Korean. There are also Koreans who have naturalized, and some children of Korean–Japanese intermarriages have become Japanese nationals too.

Almost one percent of the 120 million people in Japan are either North or South Korean nationals or Japanese nationals of Korean descent; this is contrary to the so-called homogeneity claims of Japan.

The majority of Koreans are in Japan due to the Japanese colonization of Korea. After the annexation of Korea in 1910, Koreans were forced to become the subjects of Imperial Japan. The occupying colonial policy imposed severe control on Korea. Between the 1920s and 1930s Japan used Korean soil for rice production for export to Japan. This caused severe famine and poverty in Korea and, therefore, many were despairing and left for Japan in search for jobs in order to escape the poverty at home.

Between 1939 and 1945, many Koreans were brought to Japan by force to work under hard and inhumane conditions. For instance, many young Korean women were brought to Japan to serve as "comfort women." These women had to sexually satisfy the Japanese military forces. When Japan was defeated by the Allied Forces in 1945, it is estimated that there were approximately 2,300,000 Koreans in Japan. However, many lost face even in their own country of Korea, especially the women who were used as comfort women. They had no place to go but to stay in Japan and learn to live with their circumstances.

Today, after fifty years of history, the Koreans, who make up Japan's largest minority group, have not become socially accepted. The Koreans in Japan have occasionally been viewed as "problems" by Japan's sensationalistic mass media and have yet to be recognized as close neighbors who created and nurtured a unique ethnic culture. There are many reasons for discrimination.

Koreans are considered inferior. Ethnic relationships between the Japanese and Koreans in Japan are still very poor. The Korean minority suffers discrimination in jobs, social welfare, housing, education, and social acceptance. Among Koreans in Japan, many of the elderly live alone, and the daily struggle for survival and the inability to access even basic welfare systems have left many destitute of resources for their senior years. Koreans in Japan are not qualified for any benefits from the Japanese government, and women in particular are in a difficult situation if there is no close family who can support them. Interestingly, there are many Korean Christian churches in Japan that fill the gap and provide services and help to the Korean community in Japan. Also, the church in Japan has been very active in the area of social concerns.

There are many Korean pastors and missionaries serving the Christian church in Japan; many of these churches are also visited by the Japanese Christians. In big cities such as Tokyo, there are many international churches where the Koreans, Africans, and other ethnic groups worship alongside fellow Japanese Christians.

Ethnic Minorities

In Japan, there are approximately two million foreign residents. This includes Koreans and Chinese. During the 80s and 90s, many foreign workers from developing countries came to Japan to find luck and work. Many of these newcomers are from the Philippines, Brazil, Peru, Thailand, and other nations. They came to Japan to do the jobs that the average Japanese man and woman did not want to do — the dirty and difficult jobs (kitanai) like being dead washers and construction laborers, and the dangerous jobs (kiken) like factory workers.

Immigrant women work often as hostesses, house cleaners, stripteasers, or they are working in the sex industry. There is perhaps much truth in a minority group's claim that their problems are the product of distortion and prejudice on the part of the majority of Japanese. Until 1995, Japan was among the few nations which had not ratified the International Convention on the Elimination of All Forms of Racial Discrimination that the United Nations brought into existence in 1960 (Sugimoto, 2003).

Japanese discrimination is strongly rooted in cultural beliefs. Prejudice is based on whatever is from the outside (soto) that is considered unclean, dirty, and underdeveloped. The Japanese have many cultural sayings that are loaded with prejudices. The Japanese cannot accept other ethnicities into their inner circle and treat them equally to their fellow Japanese. For a Japanese person, as long as a foreigner is a guest, whether at home or at workplace or anywhere else in Japan, they will ultimately be treated in a friendly manner by the Japanese. But once a foreigner tries to be more than a guest, the attitude of the Japanese changes drastically into an insensitive, cold and unwelcomed attitude. The Japanese have a saying *Gaijin Kusai*, which means smelling like a foreigner!

Part Three

CHRISTIANITY IN JAPAN

INTRODUCTION

Christianity has a long history in Japan. Mainstream historians believe that Christianity entered Japan in the sixteenth century with the coming of Catholic Spaniards in Japan. Some other Christian historians have a different idea that Christianity was introduced to Japan much earlier than the sixteenth century. They believe that Christianity first came to the Far East roughly 1,800 years ago along the Silk Road passing through China to Nara, central Japan. Ken Joseph Jr. is one of the most prominent researchers in Japan who has been engaged with this theory.

According to Ken Joseph Jr., one of the evidences is that the Gospel of Matthew, in old Chinese script, dates back to the ninth century and was found inside the Koryuji Buddhist Temple in Kyoto near Nara. This temple is cited by at least one historian as having been built about 818 atop a Christian building erected in 603 that was destroyed by fire. Protestantism, however, entered Japan during the Meiji Period.

In the following chapters I will be giving a brief history of Christianity in Japan up until today. Also, the condition of Christianity in contemporary Japan will be discussed. However, before discussing this topic further, I will start by dedicating some space to the main religions in Japan and how the Japanese relate to these main religions. In general, the Japanese people have a different concept of religion. There are more people registered to various Japanese religious mainstreams than the population of Japan. This means that the Japanese are registered as Buddhists while also believing in Shinto and Confucianism, and even Christianity.

In the coming chapter, I will be discussing the three main religions in Japan — Shinto, Buddhism, and Confucianism. In Chapter Seven I will focus on the history of Christianity in Japan. Chapter Eight will be about Christianity in contemporary Japan and what an average Japanese person thinks about Christianity.

CHAPTER 6

MAIN RELIGIONS IN JAPAN

Shinto and Buddhism are Japan's two major religions alongside Confucianism. These three religions have been coexisting for several centuries and have complemented each other to a certain degree.

Religion does not play a big role in the everyday life of most Japanese people today. The average person typically follows the religious rituals at ceremonies like births, weddings, and funerals. They may visit a shrine or temple on New Year's Day and participate at local festivals, matsuri, most of which have a religious background.

SHINTO

Shinto is the indigenous faith of the Japanese people and is as old as Japan itself. It remains Japan's major religion besides Buddhism. Shinto means "the way of the gods." Shinto does not have a founder or sacred scriptures like Christianity or Islam. Propaganda and preaching are not common either because Shinto is deeply rooted in the Japanese people and their traditions. Shinto gods are called kami. They are spirits that take the form of things and concepts important to life such as wind, rain, mountains, trees, rivers, and fertility. Humans become kami after they die and are revered by their families as ancestral kami.

The sun goddess, Amaterasu, is considered Shinto's most important kami. In contrast to many monotheist religions, there are no absolutes in Shinto. There is no absolute right and wrong; there is no concept of evil and good.

During the Meiji Period people were encouraged to believe and practice Shinto because this religion was strongly related to emperor worship. In Shinto belief the emperor is a god or a kami who is a lawful descendent of Amaterasu the founding goddess of Japan.

The principal objects of worship in Shinto from the earliest times until the present are the divinities known as kami. Literally translated, the word "kami" means "that which is hidden." Kami are both worshipped and venerated and include animals, birds, mountains, grasses and trees as well as historical figures and mythical figures. Kami may be good or evil. Hence, the kami of Shinto includes dragons, foxes, tigers, or tree-spirits.

During the Tokugawa Period, Shinto was subordinate to Buddhism, but due to the corruption of the Buddhist priests, Buddhism gradually lost its trust with the people. During the Meiji restoration Shinto became the national religion of Japan. This "State Shinto" has a strong ethnocentric belief that Japan is the superior nation in the world. Shinto believes that the Japanese emperor is a god himself who is to be worshiped here on earth. After World War II, this form of Shinto was banned and the emperor denounced his deity.

Three types of social organizations characterize Shinto — Shrine Shinto, Sect Shinto, and Folk Shinto. Shrine Shinto is the oldest type of Shinto and has the largest number of followers involving worship of the kami at a local shrine.

Such worship had a unifying effect upon Japanese society. While Shinto has no founder, it possesses an organization based on believers, festivals, religious practices, doctrines rooted in Shinto traditions, and Japanese myths. All these are centered in shrines and spiritual unifications (Eliade, 1987).

Sect Shinto is not as common and is a new form of Shinto. These groups were found in the nineteenth century with thirteen sects. Generally, these groups do not have shrines but instead use churches as their centers of their religious activities (ibid). These are so called new religions characterized by shamanistic leadership and philosophical beliefs.

Folk Shinto is very common in Japan among the classes with lower income. It does not have any official teachings or social organization. Rather, this type of Shinto has three sources: (1) ancient traditions such as divination, shamanistic rituals, and folk medicines; (2) basic elements such as customs of abstinence and purification rites as well as worship of house and field kami; and (3) syncretism of Shinto with beliefs from foreign religions such as Buddhism, Taoism, and Christianity.

What are the main beliefs of Shinto? Original Shinto has no theology or even a concept of ethics beyond an abhorrence of death and defilement and an emphasis on ritual purity.

Shinto creation stories tell of the history and lives of the kami. Among them was a divine couple, Izanagi-no-mikoto and Izanami-no-mikoto, who gave birth to the Japanese islands. Their children became the deities of the various Japanese clans. Amaterasu Omikami, the sun goddess, was one of their daughters. She is the ancestress of the Imperial Family and is regarded as the chief deity. Her shrine is at Ise.

Her descendants unified the country. Her brother, Susano, came down from heaven and roamed throughout the earth. He is famous for killing a great evil serpent.

The kami are the Shinto deities. The word kami is generally translated "god" or "gods." However, the kami bear little resemblance to the gods of monotheistic religions. There are no concepts that compare to the Christian concepts of the wrath of God, omnipotence and omni-presence, or the separation of God from humanity due to sin.

There are numerous other deities who are conceptualized in many forms:

- Those related to natural objects and creatures, from "food to rivers to rocks."
- Guardian kami of particular areas and clans.
- Exceptional people including all but the last of the emperors.
- Abstract creative forces (www.religioustolerance.org).

The Aspects of Kami

The kami are shadowy, formless entities that are largely devoid of personality and resemble impersonal manifestations of power. All kami are considered superior to people in knowledge and powers, holding in their gift those areas of life that are outside human control. Kami have no shape of their own. To manifest themselves, they must be summoned or cajoled into a vessel of suitably inviting form. These vessels known as yorishiro are frequently long and thin: trees, wands, banners, or long stones are common (Bowring & Kornicki, 1993).

In Japan, dolls are also believed to be residents of kami. Also, certain physically gifted people can act as mediums between humans and the kami. Most of the time women play a medium's role whereby the kami might borrow the women's body to communicate and reveal things.

Secondly, the kami are inherently non-moral. They are powers that will respond either favorably or unfavorably to the human community according to the treatment they receive. Treat them well. With proper rituals, offerings, and cult attention, they can be expected to respond with blessings in the form of good rice harvests, protection from fire, famine, diseases, and flourishing progeny.

Neglect them by exposing them to pollutions they dislike, and at once they will blast the community with tatari or curses (Bowring & Kornicki, 1993). Kami dislike pollution. By pollution I do not mean environmental pollution, but pollution in the spiritual sense caused by things that are unclean in the natural realm. Everything that is unclean may cause the pollution and most of the time the unclean is related to blood, dirt, and death. These can make things unclean and, therefore, pollute things to make the kami angry.

We have to understand that it is not moral sin that makes the kami angry but pollution. Kami are offended by blood, particularly internal blood generated at human birth and by women's menstruation and by the effluvia of death. They call the woman's menstruation "red pollution," and during this so called red pollution, they are not allowed to visit the shrines.

Those who have witnessed death in the family cannot visit a shrine for a while. Now it is clear as to why the Japanese have a certain cultural discrimination against the Burakumin or the immigrants who practice the so called dirty jobs.

In the doctrine of the Christian faith, the blood of Jesus was shed to forgive the sins of those who choose to believe in Him. Is it possible that this blood, too, will make the kami angry and, therefore, the message of the blood of Jesus is not fitting within the framework of the pollution concept that the Shinto believe in?

Lastly, kami are specialized in certain things — some in blessings for a good marriage, or good business, or conducting good study, etc. Also in Shinto, ancestors are strongly worshipped and some even turn out to be gods or kami, and all of humanity is regarded as "kami's child." Thus, all human life and human nature is sacred. Believers revere musuhi, the kami's creative and harmonizing powers. They aspire to have makoto, sincerity or true heart. This is regarded as the way or will of kami. Morality is based upon that which is of benefit to the group. "Shinto emphasizes right practice, sensibility, and attitude" (www.religioustolerance.org).

There are four affirmations in Shinto:

1. Tradition and the family: The family is seen as the main mechanism by which traditions are preserved. Their main celebrations relate to birth and marriage.
2. Love of nature: Nature is sacred; to be in contact with nature is to be close to the gods. Natural objects are worshipped as sacred spirits.
3. Physical cleanliness: Followers of Shinto take baths, wash their hands, and rinse out their mouths often.
4. Matsuri: Worship and honor are given to the kami and ancestral spirits (ibid).

Spirits of the Dead and Life after Death

The Japanese believe in spirits of the dead which are called tama. Tama reside in a host to whom it imparts life and energy, but it will detach itself in illness and leave permanently at death. It then requires nourishment by the living if it is to achieve its proper state of rest and salvation. For thirty-three years, the surviving family of the dead spirit must see that the correct kuyo or requiem obsequies are observed: food offerings, visits to the grave, and ritually powerful words. After thirty-three years, the spirit is believed to lose its individual nature and to merge with its corporate ancestors (Bowring & Kornicki, 1993).

There are dead spirits that are threats to the society. These are those spirits that are neglected within the thirty-three years. Also, spirits without any surviving families are also dangerous spirits. And lastly, there are those spirits of the people who die in violence or disgrace or those who had rage and anger in their hearts. These three types of tama are believed to wander over the earth and cause disasters and calamities.

In Japan it is believed that the dead — irrespective of the moral quality of their biological lives on earth — are going to the tops of certain holy mountains. Such mountains are recognized by their symmetrical shape such as Mount Fuji and Kiso Ontake. There is a shrine at the foot of the mountain where the dead receive ritual attention. It is believed that the dead return from these places at stated seasons to bless their families. There are the New Year and the Bon-festivals in August. The annual ancestor festivals are the seasons for welcoming back the dead.

Shinto and Christianity are quite different. In Christianity, salvation is gained by believing in Jesus Christ including His death and resurrection. In Shinto, there is no such a thing as salvation because there is no concept of sin and, therefore, no need for salvation as known in Christianity. Therefore, in Shinto there is no such a thing as judgment. For the Shinto, life after death ends up in the mountains whereas in the Christian faith life after death ends up either in hell or in heaven. Christianity believes in a triune God, one God in three entities. But with Shinto there are millions of gods. When evangelizing the Japanese people, the people may wonder which of the millions of gods Jesus is representing.

JAPANESE BUDDHISM

Buddhism originated in India in the sixth century B.C. It consists of the teachings of the Buddha — Siddhartha Gautama. Of the main branches of

Buddhism, it is the Mahayana or "Greater Vehicle" Buddhism that found its way to Japan. Buddhism was imported to Japan via China and Korea in the form of a present from the friendly Korean kingdom of Paikche in the sixth century A.D. While the ruling nobles welcomed Buddhism as Japan's new state religion, it did not initially spread among the common people due to its complex theories.

There were also a few initial conflicts with Shinto, Japan's native religion. But the two religions were soon able to coexist in harmony and even complement each other.

In 1175, Honen founded the Jodo sect or the Pure Land sect. Many from all different social classes followed this sect since its theories were simple and based on the principle that everybody can achieve salvation by strongly believing in the Amida Buddha. In 1224, the Jodo-Shinshu, True Pure Land sect, was founded by Honen's successor, Shinran. The Jodo sects continue to have millions of followers today.

In 1191, the Zen sect was introduced from China. According to Zen teachings, self-enlightenment can be achieved through meditation and discipline. Buddhist institutions were once more attacked in the early years of the Meiji Period when the new Meiji government favored Shinto as the new state religion and tried to separate and emancipate it from Buddhism.

In Japan, ninety million people consider themselves Buddhists. However, Buddhism does not directly affect or influence the everyday life of the average Japanese person. Normally, the funerals are organized in a Buddhist way, and many households keep a small house altar called a Butsudan in order to pay respect to their ancestors. In this case there is a merging area with the Shintos whereby the ancestors have to be worshipped.

In fact, ordinary people are often unaware of such a doctrine, however, they refer to their recently deceased relatives as "Buddhas" or hotoke (Hendry, 2004). Buddha means "enlightened one."

There are also differences between Buddhism and Shinto, especially when Buddhism was introduced in Japan. For instance, the Buddhist way, which sees the source of ills as being within our own minds, stood in sharp contrast with Shinto which looks entirely to the external world. The kami or deities of Shinto were thought of as bestowers of material blessings outside the competence of man, never as revealers of interior or ultimate truth. Most religious efforts in early Shinto seem to have been directed toward divine favors in this world such as a bountiful harvest and protection from famine and disease. There was no tradition in Japan comparable to Taoism in China, of spiritual methods directed to alerting inner consciousness to comprehend and expanded the mode of truth (Bowring & Kornicki, 1993). There are five precepts taught by Buddhism that all Buddhists should follow:

1. Kill no living things, including insects.
2. Do not steal.
3. Do not commit adultery.
4. Tell no lies.
5. Do not drink intoxicants or take drugs.

There are other precepts that apply only to monks and nuns. These include:

6. Eat moderately and only at the appointed time.
7. Avoid that which excites the senses.
8. Do not wear adornments including perfumes.
9. Do not sleep in luxurious beds.
10. Accept no silver or gold (McDowell, 1994).

Also, Buddhism stresses reverence for the Three Treasures which are the Buddha, the "law" or the teachings in the holy scriptures, sutras, etc., and religious community resulting in monastic organizations.

CONFUCIANISM

Confucianism is more of a philosophy than a religion. However, Japanese culture, society, and politics have been strongly influenced by this tradition which finds its origin in China in the sixth century B.C. Confucianism concerns itself with how an individual has to live in this world based on ethics and values for life. Confucianism does not focus on the journey of the soul to the next life.

Kong Fuzi, whose name was westernized by the Europeans as "Confucius," lived from 551 to 479 B.C. Confucius was a minor official who aspired to reform the violent and unstable Chinese society of his time (Bowring & Kornicki, 1993).

Confucius never claimed divinity for himself nor do his followers make such claims for him. Although it does not stress metaphysics, Confucianism is similar to other religions in its attempt to define or establish a social ethic, a worldview, a scholarly tradition, and a way of life. Confucius taught that self-enlightenment is achieved through harmony, acceptance of harmonious social hierarchy, and the functioning thereof. Therefore, society should be divided into strata and classes where everyone has a place, a function, and duties toward the family, the group, and the society. Power and position should not be abused; rather, everyone should obey authorities and the authorities should not corrupt their power.

Confucianism was imported from Korea to Japan during the fifth century. Already during the early formation of the Japanese state, Confucianism played a very important role. During the Tokugawa Period and the three centuries of stability and closed borders, Confucianism was used as a political and social worldview to organize the family, society, and the government. While Buddhism was the state religion and fulfilled the spiritual aspects of the society, Confucianism came with practical ethics to keep the society functioning. Confucian teachings covered all aspects of society and life beginning with structures and ethics within the family and its members. Father-son obedience was a very important ethic. Also, women were given categorized ranks of functions and job descriptions which they had to fulfill during their lifetimes. It seems that during the industrialization or the Meiji Period, in contrary to Buddhism, Confucianism had no problems, and it was even used as a pillar ideology of modernization and development. The influence of Confucianism is so great that even in contemporary Japan some speak of Confucionized Japan. How far this may be true varies among scholars.

I certainly believe that the Japanese emphasis on the family, paternalism, and harmony and hierarchy combined with Shinto and Buddhism has profoundly influenced the Japanese culture and society today. However, we have to realize that recently these values and ethics based on Confucian teachings are little by little losing their effectiveness.

In previous chapters, I dealt with the family and the role of women and other aspects of society. The influence of Confucianism is quite visible, but at the same time we saw the transition of these institutions including family and working life.

CHAPTER 7

THE HISTORY OF CHRISTIANITY IN JAPAN

As I have mentioned earlier, there are disagreements on when and how Christianity entered Japan. The classic historical theory, which is widely accepted by academic experts, is that Japan encountered Christianity through the Portuguese in the sixteenth century. However, due to recent discoveries, many scholars are now beginning to realize that Christianity entered Japan much earlier than the sixteenth century. In this chapter, I will be discussing both theories and after that will continue to describe further the development of Christianity in Japan during her history.

CATHOLIC CHRISTIANS: KIRISHITAN-CLAIM

It is widely accepted that Christianity was introduced into Japan in the middle of the sixteenth century. The religion was generally tolerated until the beginning of the seventeenth century, but the Tokugawa Shogunate (1603–1867) eventually persecuted its followers. When relations with the West were restored in the middle of the nineteenth century, Christianity was reintroduced and has continued to exist in Japan with varying fortunes. In 1548, Anjiro, a thirty-six year old man, fled Japan after killing someone and boarded a Portuguese ship heading to India. There he met Francis Xavier, a Portuguese priest, who was sent by the king of Portugal as a missionary to Europeans and Indians in Malacca, a Portuguese territory.

In the boat, Xavier asked Anjiro: "If I went to Japan, would the people become Christians?" Anjiro replied: "My people would not immediately become Christians, but they would first ask you a multitude of questions, weighing carefully your answers and your claims. Above all, they would observe whether your conduct agrees with your words. If you should satisfy them on these points by suitable replies to their inquiries and by a life above reproach, then, as soon as the matter was known and fully examined, the king (daimyo), the nobles, and the educated people would become Christians. Six months would suffice; for the nation is one that always follows the guidance of reason" (Francis & Nakajima, 1991).

These historical words challenged Xavier to bring Christianity to Japan. However, Anjiro somehow miscalculated and gave six months for Japan to become a Christian nation. Already more than five centuries passed and Japan was still not a Christian nation. Soon Anjiro became a Christian and was baptized, and a year later in 1549 Xavier entered Japan together with Anjiro as his interpreter.

Xavier entered Japan during the period when Japan was not yet united. There were local lords, the Daimyos, who were fighting for their territories. Some of these Daimyo welcomed the Portuguese in order to get weapons and modern technologies from them in order to use them against their rivals and enemies. The territories of these Daimyo, the Han, were in Hizen, Tosa, and Satsuma, Choshu and other Han. Some Daimyo even commanded all their people in their territories to become Christians.

Of course, this brought the anger of the non-Christian Daimyo, and they began to fight the newly converted Christians and the Daimyo.

Two years later, after his entry to Japan, Xavier left Japan for India and recruited missionaries and workers to go to Japan to evangelize the Japanese.

Between the year 1549, when Xavier entered Japan, and 1595, approximately 300,000 Japanese became Christians, among whom there were seventeen local lords or Daimyo (Best, 1966). This is the classical and well accepted theory of how Christianity came to Japan.

THE CHURCH OF THE EAST: THE KEIKYO-CLAIM

A recent discovery in Sian, China has dramatically changed the historical record of China and Asia. Asia, with China and Japan in particular, are thought of as predominately Buddhist areas. The record of the Church is very limited throughout Asia with the exception of the Philippines and Korea. As amazing as it may seem, the oldest Christian site in Asia has been dated back to A.D. 638. The site, which is near the ancient Chinese capital of Sian, has shattered the previous understanding of the role of Christianity in China, Japan, and Asia. The Nestorian Monument, a stone tablet in the city of Sian, which was discovered in the 1600s, was the only testimony of Christianity in China. What was always a puzzle was that it clearly stated that "monasteries abound in a hundred cities". This monument, which is often called the "Rosetta Stone" of Christianity in Asia, was the only proof of this past (Joseph Jr., 2001). Therefore, according to this alternative theory, Christianity entered Japan in much earlier times than Francis Xavier's arrival in Japan. The root of this theory begins in China.

For thousands of years China and the Middle East region had a strong trade relationship which all took place around and along the famous Silk Road. The Silk Road covered a vast length of trade road which covered Israel, Turkey, Iraq, Persia or Iran until China and Korea ended up in Japan. Along this trade road not only commercial goods and trade materials were exchanged but also scientific knowledge such as medical knowledge and architectural knowledge. At the same time, various forms of faith and belief were also entering China and Far Asia. One of them was the Christian faith through Nestorian missionaries who represented the Assyrian Church of the East. The pioneer of this was a certain man from Iran called Alopen, the Persian bishop who began the Nestorian mission in Chang-an in

A.D. 635 during the T'ang Dynasty. Chang-an, the upper capital, was the centre of imperial splendor. Caravans brought with them traders and jugglers, monks and pilgrims, from Persia, Armenia and even from Antioch and Byzantium. Their strange appearances and outlandish clothes never failed to amuse the Chinese onlookers. Meanwhile, the Chinese had also been deported to Central Asia to garrison the fortifications across the steppes. Against such a setting, Nestorian Christianity first came to China (Lee, 1971). Some even believe that Christianity entered China and then later on came to Japan much earlier than even the Nestorian Bishop Alopen. Studies show that as early as A.D. 86, or the third year under the reign of Yuanhe of Eastern Han Dynasty, Christianity entered China.

When studying a batch of stone carvings of the Eastern Han Dynasty (A.D. 25–220) stored and exhibited in the Museum of Han Stone Carvings, a Christian theology professor was greatly surprised by some stone engravings demonstrating Bible stories and designs of early Christian times.

Further studies showed that some of these engravings were made in A.D. 86, or the third year under the reign of Yuanhe of the Eastern Han Dynasty. Five hundred fifty years earlier the world accepted the time of Christianity's entrance into China. Members of The Church of the East have long believed that the Apostle Thomas first brought the Gospel to China through India as early at A.D. 64 and Japan in about A.D. 70 (www.keikyo.com). I believe this does not indicate that Thomas himself traveled to Japan, but rather the people and offspring of those whom he led to Christ in India brought Christianity to China and from China to Japan.

The story behind the Keikyo Christians is very interesting. I personally believe in this theory that Christianity arrived much earlier in Japan than Francis Xavier's time. However, it depends on the reader to decide which claim to choose. If one is interested, there are fascinating books and websites on Keikyo Christians and the spread of Christianity through Assyrian and Persian missionaries in China and Japan. The first interesting book is the one written by Ken Joseph Jr., called "Lost Identity," available for free on the internet in PDF format. In this book Ken Joseph Jr. describes, and historically proves through documents, archeological findings that Japan was once a Christian nation or had a Christian identity far before the arrival of

Francis Xavier in the sixteenth century. He also claims that some parts of Japan were once multicultural societies. He even claims that some cities such as Kyoto were built with the immigrants who came to Japan to settle and work. Their cultures and habits mixed with the native inhabitants of Japan.

Another interesting book is the one written by Shiu Keung Lee in the early 1970s. In this book, The Lotus and the Cross, Lee claims, just like Ken Joseph Jr., that Christianity came to Japan through Nestorian believers, those from the Church of the East. He also discusses how the Iranian bishops spread Christianity in a rapid way. Many temples were built for worshiping Christ which later were burned down or taken away by the Buddhists. Also, the website of the Keikyo Institute gives a variety of information about the early Christians in Japan.

Which Claim to Believe?

The question of which claim to believe depends on how the reader views Christianity and from which point of view the reader is looking. If Catholicism is considered as the only form of Christianity, or a superior form of Christianity, which is strongly western-oriented, and rooted in Southern Europe, then the answer is yes! If Catholicism is considered as one form of Christianity, and that Christianity is not only a western faith, but one born in the Middle East, then the second claim, the Keikyo-claim, could be a possibility.

Christianity may have entered much earlier than what Catholics claim. Of course, later on, during the Meiji Period, another form of Christianity entered Japan — Protestant Christianity, which will be discussed later in this chapter. However, let us now see how Christianity developed during the Tokugawa Period.

CHRISTIANITY DURING THE TOKUGAWA PERIOD

As I mentioned earlier in this chapter, Xavier entered Japan during the period when Japan was not yet united. There were local lords, the Daimyo, who were fighting for their territories. Some of these Daimyo welcomed the Portuguese in order to get weapons and modern technologies from them so they could use them against their rivals and enemies.

I also mentioned that between the year 1549, when Xavier entered Japan, and 1595, approximately 300,000 Japanese became Christians among whom there were seventeen local lords or Daimyo. The first thing Xavier and his companions did was to translate the catechism into Japanese by the help of Anjiro, the man who became a Catholic after he met Xavier on the ship while running away from Japan because of the murder he had committed. The missionaries began to preach by reading the Japanese catechism. The first Japanese catechism included the creation — the creation of heaven and earth by God, the fall of the angels, the creation of Adam and Eve, Noah's flood, the building of the tower of Babel, the beginning of idolatry, the destruction of Sodom, the ugliness of Sodomy, the preaching of Jonah in Nineveh, the history of Joseph the son of Jacob, the captivity of the sons of Israel in Egypt and their liberation by Moses, the commandments on Mount Sinai, the entrance of the Jews into the promised land, the fall and penance of king David, the prophet Elisha, Judith and Holophernes, the statue of Nebuchanezar, the prophet Daniel, the incarnation, an extensive description of the life and sufferings of the Redeemer, His resurrection and ascension, His return at the time of the last judgment, the reward of the good in everlasting bliss of heaven, and the punishment of the wicked in the eternal torments of hell.

Xavier provided an especially detailed description of "the creation of the world and immorality of souls, the necessity of the incarnation of the Divine Word as a remedy of his, the life, sufferings, and death and resurrection and glorious ascension of Christ our Lord" (Higashibaba, 2001).

Xavier and his companion, Fernandez, preached loudly in the streets and told their listeners how the Japanese sinned seriously in three things. First, they forgot Dainichi or the Almighty God and instead they worshiped the devil in wooden objects, stones, and senseless things. Second, they committed the sin of sodomy, a grievous and hateful sin that caused a great punishment to be inflicted upon the world of the Lord of heaven and of earth. And third, the women performed abortions and infanticides to avoid the obligation of rearing children, which was the greatest cruelty and inhumanity (ibid).

However, it is not clear how accurate the catechism was translated and how clear the message got through to the people. Of course, the message Xavier preached challenged almost all aspects of Japanese culture in those days. Despise all this, 300.000 people became Catholic Christians and accepted the message. They developed their own Christian lifestyle in Japan. Soon, some believers were trained to become what was called dojuku, or assistant-priests. In the absence of the priests, religious duties were entrusted to dojuku who helped out around the churches and the priests' residences and were also called to preach, catechize, and instruct Christians. They did not take religious vows but they shaved their heads and wore a kind of cassock devoting themselves to the service of the church (Harrington, 1993).

Persecutions and the Hidden Christians (Kakure Kirishitans)

Things began to change when politics got more involved, when certain Daimyo tolerated the Catholic Christians and allowed them to practice their faith in order to get military knowledge and weapons. This aroused the envy and the anger of the rival Daimyo who used Buddhism and Shinto as a counterfeit to the Christian Daimyo.

In the beginning Hideyoshi favored Christians. However, the rivalry between the Christian groups themselves and the coming of the Protestant Dutch traders changed this situation. In 1587, Hideyoshi realized the extent of the Christian influence in Kyushu. He, therefore, abruptly ordered missionaries to leave the country. His edicts were neither obeyed nor enforced, but they marked the end of favorable reception. In the meanwhile, Hideyoshi began to unite the Daimyo and later handed the united Daimyo over to Ieyasu Tokugawa who, in 1603, became the first Shogun.

The persecution was based on social and political factors rather than purely religious factors. The Christian exclusive claim of being the only true faith, with its unwillingness to tolerate other religions, aroused resentment in some circles. Missionaries were regarded as a potential fifth column preparing the way for Portuguese and Spanish colonialism. Since the Tokugawa Shogunate chose isolation from the foreign world, the Shogunate was on the alert for any coalition of disaffected elements that might threaten its sovereignty.

Soon Christianity was viewed as a major threat. Therefore, persecutions took serious forms that caused thousands of martyrs in Japan, and the Church began to hide. Missionaries were deported, some were killed, and many newly converted Christians remained fatherless with no guidance from the experts. On January 27, 1614, Ieyasu Tokugawa's son, Hidetada, issued another edict banning Christianity. This edict demanded the immediate deportation of all foreign missionaries, and the local Daimyo were instructed to destroy Christian churches and to force Japanese Christians to return to their national religions (Harrington, 1993).

Also, rewards in silver were paid to betray Christians and hand them over to government officials. To betray a priest was rewarded with 200 to 500 pieces of silver. Reporting a brother was rewarded with 100 pieces of silver and a dojuku with 50 pieces of silver. With this verdict things became hard for Christians. They began to hide, and this gave birth to one of the fascinating phenomena in Christian history: Kakure Christians or better said, the "hidden Christians." In various parts of Japan there were Christian communities and even villages which maintained their Christian faith for almost three hundred years and were not discovered by the authorities until they showed up in the Meiji Period. These hidden Christians were isolated from outside the Christian world and for almost 250 years they developed their own ways and manners, ceremonies, and religious practices. This issue has fascinated many scholars and historians both in Japan and outside Japan.

Organized Persecution

Going back to the persecutions, the Tokugawa regime hardened its policy towards Christians. In 1640, a special office called Kirishitans Shumon aratame-yaku, meaning Christian Suppression Office (CSO), was established to persecute Christians systematically. The CSO developed four major techniques to find the hidden Christians in the society. The first one was the reward system which I described earlier. The second technique was to make all the Japanese residents become official Buddhists and force them to register their names in the local or regional Buddhist temples. Not doing so or rejecting to do so would cause punishment and even the death penalty. The third method was the so-called kumi-method. Kumi consisted of five or more households who kept order on a local level. These kumi were obligated to report any hidden Christians to the authorities. Not doing so or failing to do so caused them to be strongly punished together with the Christians.

The last method was a certain ceremony called the "picture trampling ceremony" or in Japanese "e-bumi ceremony." All the citizens of Japan were obligated to trample on a sacred Christian image, like a cross, the Virgin Mary, or an image of Jesus Christ.

Later on, for economic reasons the paper images were replaced with metal medals which lasted longer. Consequently, these ceremonies took place in order to detect Christians, and so Japan trampled on Christ image through its streets and the alleys of every city, town, and village. Many died because they rejected to do so and chose to die as martyrs.

Martyrs of Japan

The Japanese soil has witnessed the bloodshed of thousands of Christians, especially during the Tokugawa Period. February 5, 1997 is memorialized as the 400th anniversary of the Christian Holocaust in Japan in which approximately one million indigenous Japanese Christians were slaughtered for their faith during the 250 years of the Tokugawa Period. It all began on February 5, 1597. On the hills of Nagasaki the blood of twenty-six martyrs for Christ were shed. These twenty-six individuals, ranging from 12 to 64 years of age, were stretched out and crucified upon crudely built crosses. This slaughter marked the beginning of a nearly 250-year nightmare that decimated the Christian church in Japan, which at that time, according to A History of the Christian Church in Japan by Dr. Richard Drummond, was "the largest single organized religious community within the nation."

Today, only about three Japanese in a thousand claim to be Christians. Five children ranging in age from 12 to 19 were among those killed on February 5.

Ibaragi Kun from Kyoto, at age 12, the youngest of the group from Kyoto, was admired until the end for his remarkable courage in the face of death. Shortly after the Christians were led to the place of their execution, an official came to him and begged him to recant his faith. Young Ibaragi Kun looked his tormentor squarely in the eye and replied, "Sir, it would be better if you yourself became a Christian and could go to heaven where I am going. Sir, which is my cross?" The stunned official pointed to the smallest of the crosses on the hill. Ibaragi Kun ran forward, knelt in front of his cross, and embraced it like a friend. Along with the others, he sang praises until he could sing no more (www.keikyo.com).

CHRISTIANITY DURING THE MEIJI PERIOD

During the Meiji Period, Japan opened her borders to the outside world and many things began to change. The situation of Christians also began to change. It was during this period, especially after the new religious laws of 1873, that Christianity became officially permitted in Japan.

Also during the Meiji Period, the Protestant form of Christianity was introduced to Japan. The formation of Meiji Protestantism was a part of the Meiji restoration of the late nineteenth century which I have described in Chapter Two.

Amidst the transformation and political turmoil and important decisions that policy makers were confronting, Japanese Protestantism emerged. Politically, Christianity was still considered an intruding faith, strongly related to colonizing Western nations. Thus, the authorities were careful in their dealing with Christians. Despite this, the Protestant missionaries first arrived in Japan in 1859. The missionaries, however, were restricted to a few large cities. For the Japanese, themselves, Christianity was still a banned religion (Lande, 1989).

Protestantism was organizationally transmitted to Japan through two channels. The first was through mission boards and church agencies.

The first missionaries sponsored through this "channel" set their feet on Japanese soil in 1859. They represented the Western missionary movements in organized form. They were not invited but intruded themselves upon Japanese soil.

Through another type of channel, however, Protestants were invited or offered employment by Japanese agencies. Reverend G.F. Verbeck, one of the first missionaries, was for a considerable period employed by the Japanese government.

He functioned in various capacities as an advisor. Several persons, arriving in the country as government-employed instructors, exerted a profound influence upon Protestant history (ibid).

The Converts

The converts during the Meiji Period can be classified into two groups, the Samurai converts and those from the farming class. The majority of the early Protestant converts were from the Samurai class.

The Samurai class was more open to Christianity since their kids attended western schools and were more in contact with the westerners than other Japanese people. Also, they had access to the Bible in the Chinese language and had already read it.

Like the Samurai, the farmers were searching for modern knowledge and a new lifestyle to meet the demands of the changing world. The converts found in Christianity a new socio-ethical concept which emphasized the equality of all humanity, created by God and redeemed by Christ. This concept was accepted as the gospel by those who had been thought of as inferior to the warrior class in the feudal age (ibid). Lastly, the converts saw Christianity as the fulfillment of Confucianism.

Many of these converts were zealous and on fire for their faith. Verbeck writes, "After a week or two the Japanese for the first time in the history of their nation, were on their knees in a Christian prayer-meeting, entreating God with great emotion, with the tears streaming down their faces, that he would give his Spirit to Japan as to the early church and to the people around the apostles... As a direct fruit of these prayer meetings, the first

Christian church was organized in Yokohama on March 10th 1872" (Lande, 1989).

Modernization and Christianity

The question arose: which path should Japan take in her modernization? The majority believed in western technology, but another group, which was the minority, believed that Japan should be modernized through the Christian faith.

Some Japanese intellectuals strongly promoted Christianity and somehow adopted it to the Japanese situation. Among these men, one of them was J.H. Neesima who had an outstanding personality. He was from the Samurai class and was converted to Christianity and had the opportunity to study theology in the United States. His dream was to modernize Japan through the Christian faith. Upon his return he founded the Doshisha School, which later became one of the outstanding universities in Japan.

Christians in Japan supported, directly or indirectly, the modernization of Japan in various areas, especially education. Missionaries were invited or on their own came to Japan to educate the young concerning language and other sciences. But these teachers had at the same time the opportunity to witness to the Japanese. There were many schools that gained significant influence in the society.

The other influence was the rapidly increasing importance of Christian women in society. Many organized women's groups, large and small, national and local, Christian and non-Christian, were active factors of society. And the most active members of them were Christian women, or at least what we call "sympathizers with Christianity" because until quite recently the higher modern education of women was done solely by Christian missionaries. Gradually, the sympathy towards Christians began to slow down and they were under strong tension. When J.H. Neesima, a respected Christian teacher, rejected to bow down to the Imperial Seal in the presence of a thousand students and sixty teachers, this caused a huge humiliation since the authorities considered the emperor as a god. Tensions began to grow; some schools were closed down.

Catholicism during the Meiji Period

The Catholics mainly focused on regaining the three hundred year long hidden church, the hidden Christians. Some were converted back to Catholicism, but many also remained as they were practicing their own developed way of worship. It was too hard for them to suddenly adopt their Christian rites to the Catholic way. Therefore, the Catholics called those hidden Christians, "the separated ones!"

Lastly

We have to realize that Protestant Christianity had various denominations like Methodism, Presbyterianism, and Evangelicalism. However, the Pentecostal movement was also introduced in Japan, and there were strong revival meetings. Yet we do not know much about these meetings. It would be interesting to find out how the Pentecostal movement, the fastest growing movement, hit Japan.

CHAPTER

8

CHRISTIANITY IN JAPAN TODAY

Christianity has not flourished in Japan as it has in some of Japan's Asian neighbors, particularly China, South Korea, and the Philippines. In Japan, Christianity is still considered a foreign creed that is not suitable for ordinary Japanese.

Practicing Christianity in Japan has not always been easy, and sometimes it is quite frustrating. For most Japanese, there is the idea that if you have become a Christian you have given up part of your "Japaneseness." "Going Christian" is often viewed as a betrayal of Japanese culture. Christians are often perceived as "anti-social" or "selfish" for breaking the harmony of the family unit by not observing many traditional Shinto and Buddhist rituals, especially that of praying to spirits and recognizing the dead. Many believe that the Christian faith means the West which does not best fit into Japanese culture.

However, while the Christian church is tolerated, the Christian faith does not belong in Japan. Currently, a mere 0.22 percent of Japan's population attends Christian services, and total church attendance was up by only 1.5 percent recently. Such trends are prompting serious concerns about the future of the Christian church in Japan. Rumor has it that in twenty years nearly half of the churches will be vacant and for sale since Japan's elderly membership will have passed away with no young people to replenish the churches.

Furthermore, attracting new members is like trying "to draw water with a bamboo basket" (an old Japanese proverb). The future is now as far as the 9,000-member Reformed Church in Japan (RCJ) is concerned. If the 53-year old denomination is to survive, it must instill the gospel in young members whose leadership can take the foundation of Japan's reformed faith. It must overcome the weaknesses and go forward into the new century (Moni, 2004).

GENERAL INFORMATION

During the 80s and 90s, with less than 1.5 percent practicing Christians, Japan is considered as one of the most unreached people groups in the world. Catholics, Protestants, Independents, Anglicans, Orthodox, Evangelicals, Charismatics and Pentecostals are the Christian groups that can be found in Japan today. Currently, Pentecostals, with 3.4 percent, are the fastest growing church in Japan followed by Anglicans with 1.6 percent growth. Together, Evangelicals and Charismatics have 1 percent growth. However, the average for all Christian groups is only 0.1 percent growth. On the national level, a growth of 6.1 percent a year makes Islam the fastest growing faith in Japan (Johnstone & Mandrijk, 2001). Islam is probably growing because of immigrants coming to Japan for work and not because of conversions. According to statistical calculations, with an annual growth of 0.1 percent it will take seven hundred years for Japan to double its Christian population which is now approximately two million people. Despite such numbers and statistics during the 80s and 90s, there is hope in post-modern Japan, the Japan of the 21st century. A recent poll done by Gallup Research Group, expresses certain signs of hope. According to the poll, 6 percent of Japan's population now claims to be Christian. The Gallup researchers were surprised by the high numbers of teens who claimed to be Christians (Christian Examiner Online, 2006). "In my 50 years of polling, there has been no study that I would consider as important as this one, because it provides insight into a fascinating culture," George Gallup Jr. said in a news release (ibid).

The View on Christianity

As I mentioned earlier, the Japanese people consider Christianity as a foreign religion. Because of historical and political backgrounds, the Christian faith has been related to the bitterness of the past such as colonialism and the hidden agenda of the West to infiltrate Japan. Also the Hiroshima and Nagasaki atomic attacks, which were committed by the United States, a western superpower, confirms this way of reluctant attitude and thinking towards Christianity. The lack of interest and sometimes ineffective evangelism has resulted in an unawareness concerning what the Japanese people view as Christianity. The Japanese people view Christianity as an adopted entity into certain ceremonies in Japan, like Christmas where people decorate Christmas trees and buy presents for each other.

The Japanese modern weddings are also considered as so-called Christian weddings whereby the couples marry in the "church" where women are dressed up in white and men in a suit. However, all of these may be elements of western culture but are not the elements of the true Christian faith. The Japanese people have adopted these cultural elements into their lives but not the real message and essence of the gospel of Jesus Christ.

Amidst of all this, demographically, the Japanese church is becoming old. There are too many old people in leadership of the churches today, and not all of the old aged leadership in the church are able to relate to the youth in Japan or even cope with the modern age of high-tech developments in their nation.

Currently, the average age of a pastor in Japan is approaching sixty years. Seventy five percent of the pastors are over fifty-five. There are more pastors active in the church in Japan that are past eighty than there are those under thirty (www.asianaccess.org).

Secondly, the Korean immigrants have been very active in church planting and the evangelization of the Japanese. However, due to racial issues that I have described before, it is difficult to attract more Japanese to the Christian faith.

One thing I have personally noticed when I travel to Japan is that there are upcoming international churches, some led by the Japanese and some by immigrant pastors from Asia and Africa. These churches are mixtures of Filipinos, Africans, other Asians and even Europeans. Could it be that these immigrants will be influencing the future of Christianity in Japan? Due to the low birth rate soon Japan will be confronted with marriage problems. There will be not enough potential partners for the young to marry. Will it be that the Japanese will lose their so called homogeneity and marry people from other races and with many immigrants who profess Christianity? How that would affect the church in Japan is a very interesting subject for research on its own.

Some Barriers

One of the greatest challenges that Christians face is that of seeking to proclaim Jesus Christ as the one true and living God. Many Japanese would be happy to embrace Him as another great teacher. However, they consider the claim of deity concerning Christ to be arrogant and offensive.

The second factor is the Japanese concept of religion. As I mentioned before, in Japan people believe in many kami or many gods. These gods do not have any concept of evil or good, right and wrong. In contrast, Christianity is a faith of right and wrong, good and evil. Therefore, it is difficult for the Japanese to believe in only one God.

Thirdly, the invasion and capitulation of Japan by the allied forces including the Americans and the process of democratization forced the Japanese emperor to deny his deity. The Japanese people considered their emperor as a kami, a direct descendant of the sun goddess, Amaterasu Omikami. The fact that western nations and so called "Christian nations" have forced the emperor to deny his deity may still be remembered and disliked by many older Japanese people.

Lastly, the working style of Japan and the extensive demands of the Christian faith to visit Sunday services do not match each other. The working pressure and lack of family time make it difficult for Japanese Christians to go to church on Sundays.

Part Four

JAPANESE CULTURE & CHRISTIAN FAITH

INTRODUCTION

Japanese culture is a very complex subject, and it is impossible to describe this culture within the limitations of a few chapters. The complications increase when we study this culture within the context of the Christian faith which has its own culture and values.

In the coming chapters, I will be discussing some of the important elements of the Japanese culture and place them within the framework of the Christian faith. I will then discuss what I believe is the real cultural barrier for the growth of Christianity in Japan. I will discuss how Christianity could function within these cultural frameworks in order to make Christianity much more accepted in Japan. Before dealing with the Japanese culture, it is very essential to dedicate Chapter Nine to what I define as Christianity. Thereafter, in Chapter Ten, I will be describing the Japanese cultural elements and compare them with Christian values.

CHAPTER 9

CHRISTIANITY DEFINED

What is Christianity and what makes this religion so unique? Christianity knows at least a few hundred various forms which differ from each other on doctrinal and practical matters. Some differences are small while others are very significant. During the twentieth century, Christianity expanded dramatically and became a truly global religion. According to the World Christian Encyclopedia there are about two billion Christians in the world today.

Philip Jenkins, a well-respected historian, wrote an incredible book, The Next Coming Christendom. In this book he describes interesting information and mind-blowing discoveries. His interview with the Ethics and Public Policy Center on July 23, 2003 is quite a diligent summary of his book. Philip Jenkins said the following:

Of Christians, about 550 million live in Europe, including the historically Orthodox Christians and those from the former Soviet Union. Latin America is not far behind with 470 million. Africa has about 360 million, Asia about 300 million, and North America including counting Mexico about 280 million. Tracking these numbers historically, you see that the share of Christians living in the global south has risen fast since 1900. In that year, for instance, about one in ten Africans was a Christian, and there were about 100 million Africans. Today, almost every other African is a Christian, and Africa has more than 700 million people. In both relative and absolute terms, that's dramatic growth. This means that over the next twenty-five to fifty years, Christianity will become mainly a religion of Latin America and Africa, including the African immigrants in the Americas and Europe. By 2050, only about one out of every five or six Christians will be a non-Latino white. In addition, the kind of Christianity that we are seeing in the global south is rather different from what we are used to in much of the global north. Southern Christianity is much more charismatic and believes intensely in signs, wonders, dreams, trances, visions, and-above all-healing. In all the varieties of so-called fundamentalism that are growing around the world, often in places where there is no access to modern medical care, healing is central. The success of southern Christianity at drawing new adherents is striking.

Take the case of Africa: for most of the last five centuries, Islam dominated that continent. Yet Christianity overtook Islam, and did so just yesterday-beginning in the 1960s. As I mentioned earlier, as recently as 1900 Christianity occupied a fairly marginal position in Africa. In about half a century, Christianity reversed the trend of half a millennium and became the leading religion in Africa.

The situation in Asia-the world's largest continent and home to about half the human race-is harder to summarize. Persecution is a huge problem. Christian believers and communities must hide their identities. How many are there? The World Christian Encyclopedia gives high-end estimates; I prefer the lower figures, just to be safe. The Communist government says there are around 22 million Christians in China, so we know there are at least that many: Beijing is not going to exaggerate the number of Christians. Everyone knows that there are many unregistered churches and unregistered or secret Christians. Estimates run as high as 100 million; I lean toward a figure of about 50 million. Even the low-range figures signal a lot of growth, most of it in just the last twenty years or so. Documents that leaked out in the 1980s suggested that in some areas there were mass defections to Christianity, and that converts included Communist Party officials. I think Beijing is worried (Jenkins, 2003).

What makes Christianity so popular in various parts of the world, especially in the southern part of the globe? What makes it work? The answers are to be found in what happened during the past century, especially starting with an incredible event called the birth of the Pentecostal movement in 1906. How the Pentecostal movement started or which date or place indicates the official birth of this movement is a subject of discussion and disagreement among scholars, However, the great majority of scholars and Christians believe that this movement started in 1906 in Azusa Street in California by a group of African-American believers headed by William Seymour, a son of an ex-slave. What happened? During a service in this building, the people experienced an extraordinary phenomenon; they began to pray in "tongues," the language of the Holy Spirit.

They were rolling on the ground and praying in languages and sounds that they did not understand. They believed in the sign of the Holy Spirit filling His people with power. They called this the experience of Pentecost just like what happened on the Pentecost day in the book of Acts in the Bible: "When the day of Pentecost came, they (the disciples) were all together in one place. Suddenly a sound like the blowing of a violent wind came from heaven and filled the whole house where they were sitting. They saw what seemed to be tongues of fire that separated and came to rest on each of them. All of them were filled with the Holy Spirit and began to speak in other tongues and the Spirit enabled them" (Acts 2:1–4, emphasis added).

During this event, the disciples were filled with the power of the Holy Spirit and they were bold enough to address the people outside who were astonished with what they saw. Peter addressed the people and said: "Fellow Jews and all of you who live in Jerusalem, let me explain this to you; listen carefully to what I say. These men are not drunk, as you suppose. It's only nine in the morning! No, this is what was spoken by the prophet Joel: 'In the last days, God says, I will pour out my Spirit on all people. Your sons and daughters will prophesy, your young men will see visions, your old men will dream dreams. Even on my servants, both men and women, I will pour out my Spirit in those days, and they will prophesy. I will show wonders in the heaven above and signs on the earth below, blood and fire and billows of smoke. The sun will be turned to darkness and the moon to blood before the coming of the great and glorious day of the Lord. And everyone who calls on the name of the Lord will be saved.'" (Acts 2: 14–21).

What happened at Azusa Street was believed to be the same experience that the disciples experienced on the day of Pentecost. For this reason they call this the Pentecostal movement.

THE IMPACT OF THE PENTECOSTAL MOVEMENT

The Pentecostal movement changed the course of Christianity. Soon Azusa Street received international attention and the movement started to spread to all North America, Latin America, Europe, Africa, and Asia. In less than two years, Azusa Street reached twenty-five nations such as India, China, Japan, Angola, South Africa, and more. Inevitably, one can say that the Pentecostal movement was birthed from the African–American immigrant culture of the nineteenth century (Lee, 2008). This is rapid growth!

Now let us go back to the main question, Why would Christianity grow so rapidly in the southern part of world, even becoming a non-European or non-white faith? We have to realize that today a new type of Christianity is growing in these nations of the south, or the developing nations, and that is the various forms and kinds of Christianity which were birthed out of the Pentecostal movement in 1906. Of course, within a movement there are always many other movements. During the past century we witnessed the Pentecostal movement, the Evangelical movement, the Charismatic movement, the Renewal movement, and the Catholic-Charismatic movement.

However, despite their doctrinal differences, I believe that all these movements are non-traditional Christian movements, meaning not old fashion Reformed churches, or Catholic churches, or what we call Orthodox churches. This segment of non-traditional Charismatic Christianity is rapidly growing in the world today and especially in the developing nations. There are various reasons for this positive growth.

First of all, non-traditional Christianity is open to miraculous and signs and wonders. It professes and practices healings and miracles. Since the people in the southern part of the world have different values and already have a background of spirituality, non-traditional Christianity easily can be accepted and even adopted. The Africans were already practicing spiritual rituals and even witchcraft. They were already used to spiritual things and now there comes a genuine powerful force of non-traditional Christianity. It surpasses other practices and makes the people believe in Jesus Christ as Lord and Savior. Somehow, in some cases, it becomes dangerous when traditional practices of witchcraft get combined with Christian beliefs. Especially in Africa, Asia, and Latin America we can find this kind of mixture.

Secondly, non-traditional Christianity gives proper space for women. Gender issues play an important role in non-traditional Christianity. According to Acts 2, Peter said that in the last days God will pour out His Spirit upon both men and women. Since the Pentecostal movement in 1906, women have gradually entered the scene of Christian ministry. Women can preach, teach, prophesy, pastor a church, and even today some speak of women apostles. In traditional Christianity, women were placed at home to care for their husbands and kids. They worked in the kitchen and were not allowed to teach, preach, and pray. Non-traditional Christianity has put an end to this.

As we all know, women and children are two of the most fragile and suffering people groups in the world. The rights of women and children are easily abused. The poorest people in the world are women and children. Non-traditional Christianity, in general, gives hope to women and it respects women as coequals with men. Non-traditional Christianity has a liberating message to women and their role in religion and society. The gospel of Jesus Christ is presented in a liberating way to billions of women worldwide.

Thirdly, non-traditional Christianity is open to all races and nationalities. Diversity plays an important role in this segment of Christianity. We have to be aware that the Pentecostal movement in the United States was one of the few Christian movements which united blacks and whites together. Today in the U.S. and Europe, the modern church is a colorful church made of various nationalities and races. For instance, in Africa, where there are various tribes and ethnic groups, non-traditional Christianity plays a uniting role. I was interviewing a man from Burundi. He was explaining his testimony how his friend was the head of a rebel group and there was another man who was his enemy; he belonged to the other rebel group.

Years passed and these two men met each other in an evangelistic camp meeting, this time not as enemies but as brothers. I believe these three factors are playing important roles for the growth of non-traditional Christianity in the southern parts of the world. Placing Japan in the global scenario of Christianity makes us see that Christianity is not growing in Japan. Therefore, in coming chapters I will be analyzing the elements of the Japanese culture and placing them in the context of non-traditional Christianity.

In the coming chapters, when I speak of Christianity, I do not mean "wedding someone in the church" or "decorating Christmas trees" and celebrating the "Christian New Year!" These things are considered as so called Christian culture in Japan, but in reality they are not. By Christianity I mean the non traditional Christianity whereby Christians believe in the godhood of Jesus Christ, the Father, Son and Holy Spirit and practice faith by being baptized in water and in the Spirit.

They go to church on Sundays or at least once a week and hear the message and apply it to their daily lives. The churches they visit are not traditional, and even if they belong to a traditional church denomination, they still are open to modernity and signs and wonders. And the music they use for worship is up-to-date and there are modern meetings that meet the needs of the rapidly changing world.

CHAPTER 10

ELEMENTS OF JAPANESE CULTURE

Before we can understand anyone in Japan, we have to have some idea of what their daily lives are like. This includes knowing their traditions, their beliefs, and their worldview.

There are many books and articles written and documentaries made on the subject of Japanese culture. It seems that Japanese culture has been fascinating to thousands of scholars and scientists all around the world.

It is said that the Japanese culture is very unique and consists of exclusive elements found nowhere else. I personally doubt this fact. I believe that the elements that seem very unique to Japan can be found in other cultures. For example, there are many similarities between some elements of Japanese culture and Iranian culture. For instance, the concept of aimai, means "ambiguity," "indirectness" and "not giving direct answers." Avoiding saying "no" is considered very Japanese. Japanese people tend to be indirect; this is a way of showing respect and politeness. If someone asks another person for coffee or tea, the answer will be "Both of them are fine" or "Either this or that" or "It will not matter." The very same concept is found among the Iranians. The Iranians are very indirect in some areas and through usage of words like, "perhaps," "maybe," or "it will not matter," they try to be polite and indirect.

It is also said that among the Japanese it is hard to know what they really think and what they say. What they say may be totally different than what they think. This again is strongly found in the Iranian culture. Sometimes you may not really say what you believe and think, but you smile or laugh and just agree or say things that on the inside you may not agree with or you have a different idea.

I am not suggesting that Iranian culture is totally like the Japanese for there are many differences. However, there are also similarities. I believe such similarities may be found among many different cultures, and I do not believe in the absolute uniqueness of any culture. But in some degrees every culture has its own specific elements.

In this chapter, I will be discussing some key concepts of Japanese culture, dealing with cultural values, attitudes, behavior patterns, and communication styles in contemporary Japan. Of course, I will not be able to quote all the cultural elements, but I will use certain important elements and discuss them in this chapter. Here I will systematically use the book, The Japanese mind: understanding contemporary Japanese culture, edited by Roger J. Davies and Osamu Ikedo. This book gives a clear description of Japanese culture in a simple and more understandable way. At the same time I will be looking at how these cultural elements would be forming a stronghold or a barrier to the Christian message or the opposite.

HONNE-TATEMAE

Honne means "informal, personal reality in disregard of social parameters." Tatemae means "official, public and socially required or politically correct."

Honne means an opinion or an action motivated by one's true inner feelings and Tatemae is an opinion or an action influenced by social norms. These two words are often considered a dichotomy contrasting genuinely held personal feelings and opinions from those that are socially controlled.

Honne is one's deep motive or intention while Tatemae refers to motives or intentions that are socially tuned, those that are shaped, encouraged, or suppressed by majority norms. Another dimension of this dichotomy is that Honne is expressed privately while Tatemae may be openly professed.

Observing the formalities of a business meeting, a person tends to follow protocol.

Later, while enjoying conversation with his colleagues over a glass of beer or sake (rice wine), the same person will frankly express his Honne regarding the issues raised at the meeting. Aiming at peace and harmony, the public self avoids confrontation, whereas the private self tends toward sincere self-expression.

In trying to understand Honne and Tatemae and how these contrasting concepts function in Japan, it is important to examine certain cultural characteristics such as a dislike of direct expression and the importance of harmony and ceremony in a straightforward manner for fear that it might hurt the feelings of others. So they are usually careful about what they say and they often use Tatemae in order to get along well with others.

For example, when a person is visiting someone's house in Japan and it becomes time for supper, people will often say, "Won't you dine with us?" But this is not really an invitation; rather it is a subtle hint that it is time to go home. To those from other countries this may sound confusing, but for the Japanese it is a natural way to interact socially. So the correct response to, "Won't you dine with us?" is "Thank you very much, but I am not hungry." This type of behavior is formulaic in Japanese society (Davies & Ikedo, 2002).

The Honne-Tatemae concept may sound natural in Japanese society, however, it may also cause many troubles. For example in marriage, the relationship between the husband and wife may be hindered by this concept since the couples do not say what they truly feel but act out what is required from them — a politically correct relationship. In reality, the couple may suffer inside. In Japan, the women and children are often victims of this. The Honne-Tatemae makes the Japanese people consider their worldview or their religious beliefs for themselves and they do not share them with others. Japanese Christians, especially, should be free from this concept. They may think that their faith in Christianity is something belonging to themselves, and it may not matter what they believe inside. They have to behave politically/socially correct by going along with the group and society and not sharing the gospel with other people. I surely believe that Honne-Tatemae is a cultural stronghold of Japan that keeps Christianity from being shared with others.

UCHI-SOTO

Uchi-Soto is a term in the Japanese culture used to refer to the distinction between in-groups — Uchi, "inside" and out-groups, Soto, "outside." The basic concept revolves around dividing people into in-groups and out-groups. One of the complexities of the Uchi-Soto relationship lies in the fact that groups are not static; they may overlap and change over time according to situations. Uchi-Soto groups may be conceptualized as a series of overlapping circles. One's position within the group and relationship to other groups will depend on the context, situation, and time of life. For example, a given person will usually have a family, a job, and other groups or organizations to which he or she belongs. His or her position within the various groups and relationship to other groups will change depending upon the position he or she is occupying at a given moment. Thus, a company employee may occupy a superior position within a specific company but then have a humble role in relation to the company's customers. The same employee may hold a black belt giving him or her a superior position within his or her karate club, but he or she may be a beginner at tennis and thus occupy an inferior position in the tennis club and so on.

Uchi-Soto is also associated with clean and unclean. One's house is considered clean, but outside the house may be considered as unclean and dirty. The children at an early age are learning to practice the Uchi-Soto concept; for example, the house, the class, or the school according to the level and situation is considered as Uchi. As I mentioned earlier, Uchi-Soto functions in various levels, and eventually the entire country of Japan could be considered as Uchi and the outside world as Soto (Oliai, 1997).

The Japanese generally call people from other countries gaijin no matter how long they have lived in Japan or how well they speak the Japanese language. The Japanese clearly distinguish insiders from outsiders in daily life, depending on whether the others belong to the Uchi or Soto group. This dual concept of Uchi-Soto has had a great influence on Japanese society, especially in terms of human relations (Davies & Ikedo, 2002). The Uchi-Soto concept stimulates group consciousness, and since the Japanese society is not an individually oriented society, the group plays an important role. Disturbing the group may be considered as inappropriate and impolite. For instance, it is not appropriate for the students in the classroom to ask questions from the teacher. This makes the student individualistic, egoistic, or what the Japanese call wagamama.

Or if in company, a person is ambitious and his or her acts are ambitious in order to get higher, then he may be considered egoistic and childish. This is because the person ignores the group or the Uchi for the sake of personal interest.

In relation to Christianity, Uchi-Soto could be considered both as beneficial and at the same time it may cause a hindrance for advancing the Gospel. The Uchi-Soto could be beneficial if it is used for bringing unity in the Church despite the differences in the forms and denominational practices within Christianity. The Uchi-Soto system could then be applied to create a great form of unity emphasizing the group idea and the entire related social activities connected to this system. The Uchi-Soto, however, could cause troubles due to strong "belonging to the group feelings." This can create churches and ministries that do not reach out to outsiders. In this case outsiders could also be the non-believing Japanese people and not only immigrants. The church has to realize that her doors should be open to outsiders who are willing to give Christianity a try.

The Uchi-Soto also hinders the non-Christian Japanese people from accepting Christianity as a Uchi religion since Christianity has always been considered as a Soto-faith, a western religion belonging to the "white man." At the same time, as I have mentioned in previous sections, the Japanese people are already having strong group formations and duties connected to their group. Therefore, Christianity could be a threat to the already existing Uchi groups. It is often noted that it is vital in Japanese social interaction to adopt suitable form, to know how to behave appropriately. In order to accomplish this one must define the situation correctly and in particular who the other is and where she/he belongs (Lebra, 1976).

Especially crucial is the designation of the other as belonging inside (Uchi) or outside (Soto). According to Chie Nakane, once a person belongs to a Uchi group, it is important that the person does not change it too often or else the liability of that person will be questioned and doubted (Nakane, 1973).

Jun Takimoto, a Japanese pastor and author, writes in his book, The Day the Lord Arose, the following concerning evangelism and new converts in his town Shinshiro: "There is a large fight involved when a citizen believes in the Lord Jesus Christ and confesses faith with Him. If somebody in a family becomes a Christian, he or she almost always meets up with the criticism of the entire family. When you try to stand as a Christian the harsh reality that waits for you is that you will have to overcome persecution.

If a son or daughter becomes a Christian, sometimes the parents come to the church, crying to complain, begging, 'If my daughter becomes a Christian, we won't be able to survive in our village anymore. Please, have the pastor tell her to quit Christianity.' We are in a very difficult position at times like this. There are also frequently times when the entire family will come running into the church screaming."

When believing the Lord in the midst of all of this, you have to be ready sometimes for geographic isolation, or even for being ostracized from your village ("village" refers to the neighborhood groupings that dot the city of Shinshiro — each has its own shrine, its own festival, and its own color).

The custom of "neighborhood group meetings" is deeply rooted in Shinshiro. Together with administrative business, there are many religious events, including weddings and funerals that are also conducted as part of this group.

In addition, contributions for the neighborhood shrines are also gathered through this administrative system (Takimoto, 2005).

Once again we can see that due to group forming, or in this case the neighborhood as Uchi and the expected obligations herein, it is hard for people to choose a new lifestyle, especially the one of a devoted Christian lifestyle.

This may even be the case in the majority of companies. I have mentioned earlier that some companies would not hire people who actively belonged to a religious group because the candidate is already a devoted member of a religious Uchi group. Therefore, the person's loyalty, devotion, and energy would not be one hundred percent with the company.

GIRI

Giri is the Japanese social and ethical obligation. According to Roger J. Davies and Osamu Ikedo, Giri is a key concept in understanding Japanese culture and certain characteristic patterns of behavior among the Japanese arising from traditional attitudes toward moral duty and social obligation (Davies & Ikedo, 2002).

Giri refers to the obligation a person has towards another person in the community. Giri is a task belonging to everybody in the Japanese society. Giri depends on two important variables: first the person and his or her function or position; and second, the situation where the person is involved at a certain time and place (Oliai, 1997).

Giri runs the Japanese saying, "hardest to bear." According to Ruth Benedict, Giri is a series of obligations of a different color. There is no possible English equivalent and of all the strange categories of moral obligations, which anthropologists find in the culture of the world, it is one of the most curious. It is specifically Japanese (Benedict, 1946).

"To an Occidental," Ruth Benedict writes, "Giri includes a most heterogeneous list of obligations ranging from gratitude for an old kindness to duty of revenge" (ibid). Ruth Benedict suggests that even Japanese dictionaries can hardly define it. One renders it "righteous way; the road human beings should follow; something one does unwillingly to forestall apology to the world" (ibid).

"Unwillingly" is one of the issues here. The Japanese may do you a favor even unwillingly, out of duty. Giri is expected from that person. This can be very confusing for strangers who visit Japan. Giri contains various systems of relationships such as student/master relationship and employee/employer relationship. Giri does not only function vertically but also horizontally on a peer level of relationship.

Some Characteristics of Giri

Based on Giri there are various expectations and duties a person should fulfill. Breaking these duties and expectations will make the person lose his/her face and bring shame. However, in case someone breaks the duty expected from him/her, still others should continue to practice their duty, their Giri, towards that person.

A Giri-relationship is "eternal" and, therefore, it creates continuous new duties and expectations. Giri does not know a special form of material considerations, but more affective oriented duty.

Even though, generally speaking, it is universal that social interactions are egocentric, also in Japan, however, one should at least try to show certain affections towards others even if that affection does not come from the heart and even if it is not real. Giri is strongly characterized by the hierarchical consciousness of the participants. This was definitely due to the strict social classification imposed on the Japanese people during the 250 years of the Tokugawa regime.

Lastly, with Giri there are no behavioral ethics or codes that are forces to the participant. Therefore, if someone breaks his or her duty he or she is "sinning" against his or her own Giri consciousness, and the person will be ashamed anyway. So why should there be sanctions or enforcements on the one who does not fulfill his or her Giri? Giri is rooted in Confucian ethics and social and behavioral rules. Confucianism deals with human interrelations and interactions and does not know a form of interaction between humans and supernatural beings of any form or kind. Human beings are obligated towards each other and not towards any form of god.

Giri could be implemented in the various forms of Christian social organizations and churches. Giri could somehow be used in a sense of Christian obligation towards the non-Christians in Japan. The Japanese should be trained and taught that it is their duty toward their fellow Japanese to evangelize them, probably through certain social services and support such as helping the elderly or with certain services or educational programs for the youth. Also on the individual level it should be the Giri, the duty towards the non-Christian people through affection and love.

From the other side, people are already within a certain sphere of Giri or duty, and it is very hard to break through the already existing Giri relations and create Christ-based Giri oriented social relations and interactions. In this case, Giri could be seen as a stronghold and barrier for Christianity.

AMAE

Amae, which can be roughly translated as "depending on the benevolence of others," is a key concept for understanding Japanese personality structure. Amae is vital for getting along with others in Japan and is the basis for maintaining harmonious relationships in which children depend on their parents, younger people rely on their elders, grandparents depend on their adult children, and so on (Davies & Ikedo, 2002).

The concept of Amae strongly affects all aspects of Japanese life because it is strongly connected to concepts such as Giri. Due to Amae, the Japanese have difficulties saying "no" or directly rejecting or disagreeing with someone. People hesitate to refuse others for fear of breaking the relationship or offending someone or hurting someone's feelings. This may disturb the group harmony, the Wa Wa, which can be understood as unity and harmony — "the desire to be one with those of your group." Wa is a concept that, while recognizing that people are not one thing, highlights the desire to be like one thing. In other words, although people are different individuals, for the Japanese culture, basically it is the best when they want the same thing. All in all, this deep level of sharing underpins the desire for harmony in interpersonal relations and a consideration of others within the group. Amae, therefore, is strongly related to Wa.

Even though Amae is meant to create a deep emotional bond with others within the group, it also creates distance from others outside the group. Therefore, the Japanese would not be open and may even be pessimistic towards those outside the group.

Here is an example of how Amae works, taken from the book written in Dutch which translates as Woman breaks loose: many faces of Japan, written by Kjeld Duits, a Dutch journalist who lived for years in Japan:

"The eighteen year old Naomi K. explains her relationship with her boyfriend: "Whenever we walk in the street together, I want him to hold my hands." However her feeling of Amae makes it difficult for her to take the first step and hold his hands. She wants to be one with him, but he has to feel her feelings between lines and hold her hands. "I would not take action first and hold his hands. I want him to do so. However, I cannot ask him directly to hold my hands, but I give him vague signs so that he takes the first step. I pull his jacket a bit or give him a push softly." Also Naomi wants him to call her by phone. She waits and waits. "If he did not give me a call, I can't do anything about it, then I have to call him" she says. "But I want him to call me and ask me out to go shopping. Then I will not call him and will not ask him to go out. I will wait. I want him to read between lines what I want and desire" (Duits, 2002).

Here is another example. In a business context, the indirect and silent negotiation style of the Japanese businessperson is still quite typical and well known. The Japanese are unwilling to say "no." In particular, when they say "yes" they mean "no." As Lewis describes, if you say to a Japanese, "I want you to lend me a hundred dollars," they will say "yes," without actually offering the money. What they mean is, "Yes, you want me to lend you a hundred dollars." If they do not wish to enter into a deal with a foreign partner, they will not come out with a negative reply. However, you will not be able to get in touch with your contact in that company thereafter. He or she will always be ill, on a holiday or attending a funeral (Lewis, 1996). The Japanese like doing business in a harmonious environment. They don't like to offend their business partner by displaying open and direct disagreement or refusal.

The Japanese seldom criticize each other or even third parties and they never say "no" directly. Excessive frankness is therefore usually out of place when negotiating with the Japanese merchants (ibid).

Amae is also frustrating for the other person, the one who receives the Amae with all its vague and confusing signs. A sixty-five year old office manager explains how he and his colleagues would crack their brains in order to find out what their boss was expecting from them or desired to be done. "In a hot summer day, if the boss says it's hot today, we begin to ask ourselves, 'What we should do?' and in case someone has the courage he may turn on the air-conditioning, says the office manager. After turning on the air-conditioning, the boss would not show any reaction or gives irritating comments, then we know he did not mean we have to turn on the air-conditioning. In case this does not work, says the office manager, then someone opens the window, and if that does not work then someone would give the boss an ice tea." (Duits, 2002). This would continue on and on until they find out what their boss really wanted.

In certain cases Amae contradicts some Christian values. For instance, Jesus said in the Bible: "Simply let your 'Yes' be 'Yes,' and your 'No,' 'No'; anything beyond this comes from the evil one" (Matthew 5:37). When I am speaking about Christianity here, I do not mean western culture, but pure Christian doctrine based on what the Bible indicates. Directness and being clear is one of the values of Christian faith. This is the opposite of Amae. Imagine evangelizing someone who says "yes" but means "no."

I consider Amae as a stronghold; it makes people somehow captive within the four walls of being attached and considerate to the group and not being able to display one's convictions. This can even be a stronghold within the church. If Amae consciously or unconsciously is being applied in churches and Christian fellowships in Japan, it makes it hard for them to reach the unbelievers. Could this be one of the reasons why the church in Japan is not growing?

AIMAI

Aimai means "ambiguity," which is defined as a state in which there is more than one intended meaning resulting in obscurity, indistinctness, and uncertainty. To be ambiguous in Japanese is generally translated as aimaina, but people use this term with a wide range of meanings including "vague, obscure, equivocal, dubious, doubtful, questionable, shady, noncommittal, indefinite, hazy, double, two-edged," and so on (Davies & Ikedo, 2002). In short, Aimai is an ancient method of communication for Japanese people which has its roots in the need for harmony. As I mentioned earlier, during the Tokugawa Period, Japan was cut off from the outside world. As a result, communities depended on each other to produce food. Collectively, they had to work and cooperate together in harmony in order to produce more. In order to do so they practiced Aimai.

"Natural communication often occurred without spoken words, and people followed their elders because they had more experience, wisdom, and power. In order to live without creating any serious problems for the group's harmony, people avoided expressing their ideas clearly, even to the point of avoiding giving a simple yes or no answer. If a person really wanted to say no he or she said nothing at first and then used vague expressions that conveyed the nuance of disagreement."

Another reason for ambiguity is the feeling that to speak directly is to assume superiority over the person you are conversing with. The Japanese think it is impolite to speak openly on the assumption that their partner knows nothing. The Japanese value Aimai because they think that it is unnecessary to speak clearly as long as their partner is knowledgeable. To express one's self distinctly carries the assumption that one's partner knows nothing, so clear expression can be considered impolite. Silence can also be considered a form of ambiguity. For the Japanese, silence indicates deep thinking or consideration, but too much silence often makes non-Japanese uncomfortable.

Once again we can see that being direct and not sharing the real heart but following the interests of the group plays an important role. In the case of Aimai, it also goes deeper assuming that the other person already knows what you want to say even if he or she does not know what you are talking about. This act makes the other part coequal to the speaker, or else it may look very superior and proud if someone explains everything in detail. Of course, this makes evangelism a very hard work, like assuming that they also know Christ and the good news of the gospel.

Some evangelists, especially from Northern America or Europe, go to Japan or even another country in the world with the attitude that "we" are coming to teach something, and "we" know it better and "we" have it all, and "we" come to bring "our" style of worship and serve God. This attitude makes the evangelists or missionaries look like Wagamama — childish and selfish.

However, I still consider Aimai as a stronghold because the Christian message is a direct message and cultural values such as this block the directness of the gospel of Christ to the audience. For this reason, the outsiders going to Japan for evangelism work, or even Japanese Christians, should practice directness in their message and lifestyle. The Christian leaders and pastors and those in authority have to teach the Japanese Christians the basic principles of why it is important to be direct and what directness can do when they witness to an unbeliever.

SEMPAI-KOHAI

Sempai-Kohai basically means seniority rules and regulations in Japan. In Japan, vertical relationships play a very important role, actually more than horizontal relationships. In Japan seniors are called Sempai and they address the juniors with Kohai.

Vertical hierarchies have existed since the beginning of Japanese history and are still prevalent in daily life, especially in schools where seniority rules are important.

For example, a third-year student has great power in junior high and senior high schools, and especially in clubs these relationships are important. It is common in sports clubs for Kohai to clean the rooms, collect balls, and manage the equipment for Sempai.

They must also give a small bow or say hello respectfully to their Sempai when greeting them. In general, students put much more emphasis on age than ability in Japanese schools. Seniority rules also influence relationships between teachers and students (Davies & Ikedo, 2002).

Seniority rules in Japanese relationships are also important in companies or institutions. The seniority system and the lifetime employment system are foundations of life in Japanese companies although it remains to be seen whether this structure will survive in Japan. Status, position, and salary depend largely on seniority, and older employees are generally in higher positions and are paid more than their younger subordinates (ibid). However, as I have discussed in previous parts of this book, the lifetime employment system is slowly reducing and the question is, "Will the seniority culture survive this in another form or not?" Only time will answer this.

The Sempai-Kohai system has its advantages once it is practiced properly. However, this system is not always used properly and some people abuse this cultural system, sometimes in the most extreme and even inhumane ways. Especially at schools this cultural element is strongly misused and it creates an environment for the bullying and abusing of the juniors by the seniors. Kjeld Duits describes some of these abuses in a very horrible way. Ichiro Yamada's testimony is one of them.

Ichiro's dream came to pass when he was accepted to one of the prestigious high schools in West Japan. Ichiro's ambition was to become a professional athlete in kendo, the Japanese sword fighting sport. This school, which he attended, is quite known for this sport. However, the dreams of this young man turned into a terrible nightmare from which he could barely escape. After a month of attending that school, his mother began to notice blue spots and bruises on his knees and back. She commented on that, but her son avoided answering her, or he would say that he had fallen during practice.

A month later, Ichiro came home from a sports competition and was perplexed and shocked by what he had seen in the changing room of the sports center. Three of the juniors on the team of five live in the same dormitory as the seniors. He explained how the seniors sexually and brutally harassed these three boys. Kjeld Duits described the details which I do not find appropriate to describe in this book.

Ichiro told one of the boys that he should speak to his parents, but the boy strongly refused because of what could happen to him. Within a few months, the juniors on the team began to speak about suicide and ending their miserable lives. When the story reached some of the parents, the parents went to the school and protested. One of the mothers begged and pleaded with the coach, and yet it did not help at all. Instead, the coach laughed at her and ironically said: "The times have so changed that even the parents are coming to tell me these things." Then he addressed all the parents and said: "If I stop this bullying, your kids will never win any competition." The parents begged for two hours and yet the coach did not show any sympathy and even ridiculed the parents (Duits, 2002).

According to statistics from 1999, there are 60,000 victims like the one Ichiro witnessed. Most of these incidents take place in the high schools. No wonder some kids commit hikikomori, isolating themselves for years. In this case, we can see how Sempai-Kohai plays a negative role.

Lastly

There are many other important elements to be described in the Japanese culture. I only chose a few of them to explore in this chapter. I hope these examples show how to understand the Japanese culture before trying to evangelize it. Next chapter, I will be dealing with some important spiritual cultures in Japan such as festivals and beliefs related to these festivals.

CHAPTER

SPIRITUAL CULTURE IN JAPAN

Every culture has its own spiritual beliefs and ways of thinking including how it relates to important days and traditions. Also, in Japan there are such things that I will be addressing in this chapter. The important festivals and cultural beliefs will be explained.

MATSURI: IMPORTANT TRADITIONAL FESTIVALS

Matsuri means "festival." There are various festivals in Japan. Some are nationwide and some are locally bound. Matsuri comes from Matsu, meaning "to welcome the invisible to the visible world." Matsuri's have two aspects — contact with the invisibles and also contact with the living and people. In the following I will explain some important Matsuris or festivals in Japanese culture.

Bon or Obon Festival

This festival is celebrated according to the lunar calendar. Bon, the festival of souls, is held in mid-July or mid-August depending on the area. It is believed that each year during Obon day, the ancestors' spirits return to this world in order to visit their relatives.

Traditionally, lanterns are hung in front of houses to guide the ancestors' spirits. People visit the graves and offer food at the house altars or in the temples. Special dances are performed on this day. The streets are decorated with lanterns and at the end of Obon floating lanterns are put into rivers, lakes, and seas in order to guide the spirits back to their world. The customs followed vary significantly from region to region.

Setsubun

Setsubun is held on February 3 or 4. Each year on this day people open the doors of their houses and drive the demons or bad luck out of their homes by throwing roasted soybeans around the house and shouting: "fuku wa uchi, oni wa soto" meaning "In with good luck! Out with demons."

It was started originally as an imperial event on New Year's Eve for the purpose of getting rid of demons and to welcome in the happy New Year. Later it was incorporated with the indigenous custom of throwing soybeans at the time of planting rice seedlings, and it has thus evolved into its present form (Katayama, 2004).

Hinamatsuri

Hinamatsuri is the girls' festival, or some can say the "dolls festival." This festival is celebrated on March 3 when the birth of girls is celebrated and wishes are expressed for their future happiness. Hinamatsuri is the day on which Hina ningyo, a set of dolls dressed in ancient costumes, is displayed together with peach blossoms as decorations. A sweet drink made from rice called shirozake is offered.

According to the Japanese people, the dolls have souls. An average Japanese person will never place a doll in a sleeping room since one never knows what kind of strange things the doll could perform in the night (Duits, 2002).

Some dolls in the Hinamatsuri festival are passed from generation to generation and some are a few hundred years old. They cost fortunes of money. The girls of the family inherit them. During World War II many of these dolls were destroyed. Also, in Hiroshima many were lost. That is why after the war the doll industry in Japan boomed and some doll makers made fortunes of money.

The Japanese people value dolls so much that they have to pass them over to someone or to the next generation. They never throw a doll away. The dolls have their own place in the temple where they are kept. Some are placed in small wooden boats and are released in the ocean. They take away all bad luck, illness, uncleanness, and negative thinking with them. Other dolls are burned in the temple similar to a cremation ceremony (ibid). We can see that dolls play a role of emotional healing for the Japanese and they function somewhat as little saviors for the people, taking their guilt, negative mind, and bad luck upon themselves. This is what the Japanese believe!

Each year before this festival begins on March 3, most families take their beautiful collection of dolls out of the closet around mid-February and put them away again as soon as Hinamatsuri is over. This is because of an old superstition that families that are slow in putting back the dolls have trouble marrying off their daughters.

In the display, the dolls represent the members of the imperial palace of ten centuries ago. At the top of the display are two dolls representing the Emperor and the Empress. Some of these dolls would cost more than thousands of dollars. On Hinamatsuri Day the girls are cherished. They get attention from their parents and family. They pray for the well being of their girls.

Tango no Sekku

Tango no Sekku is an event rooted in ancient times which is held on May 5 which is Children's Day. People express the hope that each boy in the family will grow up healthy and strong by flying carp-shape streamers outside the house and displaying a warrior doll. The custom, developed in a warrior class of society in the feudal era, was also observed among civilians of the time in a different way. Women are considered superior to men on that day. For example, women take a bath before men and men prepare meals for the women (Katayama, 2004). Of course this is very ironic in regard to the events that are happening in the modern society in Japan and how women are viewed in Japan.

SOME MODERN DAY EVENTS

With the emergence of the western culture in Japan after World War II, some western cultural events such as Christmas and Valentine's Day became very important in Japan. Christmas was initially introduced to Japan with the arrival of the first Europeans in the sixteenth century. But only in recent decades has the event become widely popular in Japan. This has occurred despite the fact that Christians make up only about two percent of the population. While Christmas is not a national holiday in Japan, more and more people are decorating their homes, giving presents to friends, and celebrating the event with a special meal. In a survey conducted by "Japan-guide.com," among young Japanese people a majority of fifty-four percent responded that Christmas means something special to them. Women and teenagers show a particular attraction to the holiday.

Those most enthusiastic about Christmas, however, are the retail stores and shopping malls where Christmas trees, Santa Clauses, and other seasonal decorations can be found several weeks in advance of Christmas.

Some public places also feature seasonal illuminations. The traditional Japanese Christmas food is the Christmas cake which is usually made of sponge cake, strawberries, and whipped cream. As many as seventy-three percent celebrate Christmas with a cake (www.japan-guide.com). Also Valentine's Day is for the Japanese. The girls not only have to buy chocolates for the one they love or like, but they have to buy Giri-Choco obligated chocolate to their male colleagues. Also, fathers and husbands get chocolates from the girls or ladies. One month later on March 14, the men have to do the same to the women. They call this day the White Day. On it, the men buy white chocolates for the ladies and some women also get white underwear! The men give only to those ladies whom they received something from on Valentine's Day a month earlier.

FORTUNE-TELLING IN JAPAN

Japan is a fortune-telling nation. The fortune-telling business is rapidly growing and various new forms of fortune-telling are now being invented. Fortune-tellers are also in the streets and across the subway stations. More and more people are consulting the fortune-tellers for various reasons: some for business decisions, some for finding the right partner, and some for guidance at their working places. People in Japan are searching for answers, especially during this period of time when this nation is undergoing gradual but radical social-economical and cultural changes.

Uncertainty about the future is one reason for the booming fortune-telling business. I have also discovered that people avoid going to professional psychiatrists for fear of losing face among their relatives and friends. Instead, they consult fortune-tellers, and they even base their lives upon what these fortune-tellers say.

Lastly

It seems like the Japanese festivals of inviting the invisible to bless their daughters and sons do not quite work for many kids who are being bullied at schools and the 500,000 to 1,000,000 youth being isolated in Hikikomori. In the coming chapter, I will deal with some socio-cultural phenomena which I call "socio-cultural illnesses." These illnesses are culturally and socially bound to each other and they are influencing the Japanese society to become less healthy.

It seems like the Japanese people are searching for something new — for answers. I hope the church and Christianity will fill this gap. May the church provide biblical and ethical solutions for the searching Japanese men and women.

CHAPTER 12

SOCIO-CULTURAL ILLNESS

Just like any other society, Japan has her own social and cultural illnesses. Some of these illnesses are believed to be unique or at least unique in Japan. In this chapter I will be describing some of these illnesses in order for us to give a picture of what is going on in Japan. From the previous parts and chapters of this book, I hope it is already clear that some things are not going so well in Japan and that Japan is on the edge of a tremendous social and cultural transformation. The changing role of women in Japan, the increasing divorce rate, the low birth rate, a fatherless generation, isolated youth, and changing family values are all part of these social transformations.

The growing digital industry and technology cause other types of social phenomena which sometimes lead to extreme social and cultural behavior causing social illness and moral decay in Japan. In this chapter, I categorize three major social and cultural illnesses: (1) sexual category; (2) children and youth; and (3) social behavior.

SEXUAL CATEGORY

Japan scores very high when it comes to the sex industry and entertainment. As I mentioned in Part One, since the Tokugawa regime Japan has been exposed to erotic and pornographic literature. Also, professional prostitution was already practiced since the seventeenth century in Japan.

The sex industry accounts for one percent of the Gross National Product, and it equals the defense budget. And despite the rickety economy, it's getting bigger. A recent survey by Takashi Kadokura, an economist with the Daiichi Life Research Institute Inc., found that the Japanese market for what is rather quaintly called the entertainment trade swelled to a tumescent [yen] 2.37 trillion in fiscal 2001, up from [yen] 1.7 trillion a decade earlier. This figure does not include virtual sex, Japan's huge sales of adult magazines, rentals and sales of porn videos and DVDs, and the burgeoning market for Internet porn. And let's not forget receipts from the country's estimated 40,000 love hotels.

The buying and selling of sex and sex-related services in the world's second largest economy is worth more than the GDP of many smaller countries (Macneil, 2003). The majority of the prostitutes are from other countries. There are 60,000–70,000 Filipino dancers in Japan, a third are undocumented. Filipino women are vulnerable to trafficking due to the Asian economic crisis. Requests for entertainer visas for Japan did not decline in the first six months of 1998. Travel to Japan increased twenty-one percent in the first half of this year compared with the same period in 1997. The label "entertainer" sometimes implies "sex worker." The women are vulnerable in Japan, not because they lack skills, but because they are young, beautiful women in a hazardous and vulnerable occupation. Trafficking laws exist but are not enforced (Fact book on Global Sexual Exploitation, 1999).

Pornography

In 1998, Japan was the world's biggest producer of child pornography. Parliament recently refused to pass a law banning the production of child pornography citing "business reasons." One thousand illegal pornographic tapes are produced in Japan each month with thirty-five new titles produced each day. Already, 19.3 percent of Tokyo high school boys are interested in using the Internet to access pornography (ibid).

Pornography is so pervasive even schoolchildren have access to comic books with pornographic contents. Sex magazines can be bought at vending machines. Pornography is available twenty-four hours a day through cable television. Pornography can be accessed through computer networks (ibid). Advertisements known as "pink chirashi" promoting videos and massage parlors are placed in people's mailboxes. They are legal and widespread (ibid).

Internet Pornography in Japan

In November and December 1997, a survey polled 1,928 high school and university students as well as 1,244 parents of high school students in Tokyo, Osaka, Mie, Fukuoka, and Okayama prefectures. Of students who have used the Internet several times:

- 51.1 percent of male university students and 46.2 percent of male high school students have accessed pornographic material on the Internet.
- 4 percent of female university students and 8.2 percent of female high school students have accessed pornography (ibid).

Of students who said they knew of the Internet: 80 percent responded that they were aware they could access pornographic material. Also, 66.4 percent of mothers and 60.3 percent of fathers responded that it was wrong to look at pornographic material on the Internet. The majority of parents responded that pornographic sites on the Internet should be either legally regulated or voluntarily regulated by the provider of the material. In addition, 57.8 percent of male high school students and 30.4 percent of female high school students said it is acceptable to look at pornographic materials on the Internet (ibid).

Digital Crimes

A Few years ago, when camera phones were broadly available in the United States, more than 25 million of the devices were already out on the streets of Japan. Japan leads the world in fancy mobile phones. However, these fancy phones cause the social problem of digital crimes. Men are secretly taking pictures of ladies in the streets, pools, megastores, etc. Some even sell these pictures or video clips to the sex industry either on the internet or to the video industries.

Many people, even prominent people in high ranks and positions, are addicted to this digital sickness. Japan is not the only nation with this problem. Other countries in Asia and even the United States are confronted with this problem.

Kinsuke Kageyama, a professor in criminal psycho-pathology, believes that this problem is caused by stress. "There are many middle aged men secretly glancing at women because these men are addicted to their works and they do not quite know how to deal with their stress." According to Kageyama, most of these men who do such things are respected people from the society, but they miss something in their lives and they feel they are not important people in their organizations. 'Perhaps they are trying to create a feeling of satisfaction by secretly filming other people. This act gives them a false feeling of ruling/controlling someone'" (Duits, 2002).

According to Kamon Hei, a journalist in Asahi Shinbun, a Japanese newspaper, about twenty percent of Japanese pornography videos are made by secret cameras (ibid). The law in Japan is very weak concerning secret camera pictures; the punishment for this crime is approximately $600 in United States currency. This situation is very different in the United States. According to a CNN report, in the United States secret picture taking of women may lead to a $100,000 fine and imprisonment.

Groping

In Japan, more than four thousand men are arrested each year for groping women on trains. This is about five times the number in 1992. In 2001, a survey of two private high schools in Tokyo revealed that more than seventy percent of the girls had been groped on the train. A recent survey of Japanese companies suggested that at least seventeen percent of Japanese women have been groped.

Underage Sexual Relationships

A growing number of schoolgirls in Japan are turning to prostitution so they can afford such expensive designer items as a $500 Prada purse or a $350 Louis Vuitton wallet. Tokyo Metropolitan University sociologist, Shinji Miyadi, predicted that eight percent of schoolgirls across Japan and one-third of all girls not headed for college, have joined the sex industry. Furthermore, men are turning increasingly to younger girls.

One factor related to the increase in schoolgirl prostitution in Japan is that health officials there do not express much concern about the rates of AIDS and other sexually transmitted diseases among the population. The number of cases of AIDS, HIV, and venereal disease in Japan are admittedly fairly low, but some health officials believe that the diseases could be under-reported because many people are not tested for them. "There is a possibility that many more teenagers are carriers and aren't reflected in the statistics," said Taku Kato, director of an AIDS research team at the Ministry of Health (www.aegis.com, 1996).

Teen prostitution is not shocking news. The age limit for having sex is twelve years old. These kinds of practices show us that Japan is on the edge of an increasing degeneration of morals and ethics in all facets of society.

CHILDREN AND YOUTH CATEGORY

There is a huge pressure on the youth in Japan. High expectations from the parents, the situations at home, the hard standards of schooling, and losing face when failing in school cause many youth to become stressed, depressed, and even suicidal. Many end up in long years of isolation. Here are some of the issues that have been causes for concern.

Ijime: Bullying in Japan

Bullying is a common problem in every generation and every country. In Japan, it is a fairly serious social phenomenon. Actually, the amount of Ijime, which means "bullying" in Japanese, has been decreasing. However, the bullying is getting much more sinister than before. Five years ago, it was top news for the whole year after Kiyoteru Okochi, a 13-year-old junior high school student, committed suicide to escape being bullied by his classmates. He left a note that proved and clarified the fact that he was suffering from cruel bullying.

He was often forced to soak his face in a dirty river. His bicycle was broken repeatedly, and his classmates even demanded that he bring money to them every day. The amount of money that he gave to the bullies reached about $10,000. This was not the first time that students committed suicide because of bullying. But it was the first time that the Japanese media gave a lot of coverage to the matter of Ijime. After that, bullying became one of the most serious subjects in Japan. People wondered why his classmates bullied him. There are many possible answers but none of the causes is simple.

Unlike the United States where bullying traditionally entails one or two strong students cowing a greater number of weaker students, bullying in Japan usually takes the form of a large group of students picking on or tormenting one or two weaker ones. The victims have nowhere to go. There is no professional help for this in Japan, and if there is, people refuse to go because of losing face. Fitting in a group is very important in Japan. Often the bullying ends with the victim's suicide. After the suicide there is a massive display of grief by the school and classmates who almost all deny that they knew there was anything wrong, which is not true. They know it but due to fear and cultural aspects they do not want to reveal the true story.

Hikikomori

As I have discussed in the previous chapters, Hikikomori is an increasing phenomena in Japan. Hikikomori basically means the isolation of a person, normally a young person, from the society and family. They lock themselves up in a room and do not come out for years, sometimes even decades. In his research at the University of Hawaii, Manoa, Michael J. Dziesinski discovered very interesting information and facts concerning the gradual process of Hikikomori (see Table 1) and the causes of this tragic phenomena (Table 2).

Table 1: Progression of Hikikomori.

Phase 1	Social Pressure	School, exams, family, career expectations
Phase 2	Trigger Bullying	Exam failure, embarrassment
Phase 3	Slow Withdrawal	Progressive seclusion from outside contact, from outermost peer groups inward to family
Phase 4	Parental Collusion	Parents, usually the mother, help victim withdraw owing to shame about condition and fear that neighbors will know
Phase 5	Lack of institutional Response	Schools, hospitals, and government have no apparatus to deal with victim, so they ignore the problem or commit the victim to mental care
Phase 6	Years of Isolation	Victim hides in the room and avoids social contacts
Phase 7	Rehabilitation/ Socialization	Victim is removed from environment, given purpose and social interaction

Source: Michael J. Dziesimki, 2003.

Table 2: Societal factors "causing" Hikikomori behavior.

Various Causes for Hikikomori

Family Affluence	Victim able to stay home, play video games and watch TV
Ambiguity of Male Role	Young men unsure of future in economic recession and lack male role model
Ijime, Bullying	Bullying to conform
Tokokyohi	School refusal
Exams	Failure to succeed
The Child's Room	Sacrosanct in Japanese harms
Gogatsu Byo	May-disease — not sure how to live after school years
Depression	School, clinical
Mother-Son	Co-dependent relationship in Japanese culture
Hitorikko	Declining birthrate = more single child families
Parental Expectations	School, career, exams
Media Visibility	Emulation of more serious victims
Neighbors	Family fears neighborhood finds out
Social Institutions	No structure for recognition

Source: Michael J. Dziesinski, 2003

Incest

During my research, I discovered a shocking phenomenon. In Japan, mother-son related incest is relatively higher than other countries. This goes contrary to other cultures where the majority of incest cases are father-child related. At the beginning I did not want to address this issue. However, after sincere consideration, I decided to mention it in this book. Because of the cultural setting of the Japanese society it is hard for kids to mention this easily. It is also difficult to address this issue with specific and accurate research and statistics.

According to Lloyd DeMause, the stonewalling on information about incest in Japan has been breached somewhat by four recent studies. The first is a Japanese feminist sex survey that reported that one-third of its respondents had memories of being sexually abused by relatives or close friends as children. This figure is considerably higher than comparable statistics in the United States. Secondly, other studies show that the majority of urban parents in 1981 reported that they had lately begun to be bothered by the thought that children with whom they slept might be aware of their intercourse — a growing guilt about incestuous activities that was increasingly common in the West in early modern times and which led for the first time to separate beds for children.

Thirdly, two recent books on Japanese incest provide new insights into the subject. The first is a report of a "hotline" set up in Tokyo by a counseling service which analyzed hundreds of calls they received dealing with incest. Since official Japanese statistics deny the occurrence of incest, they were surprised to find that their hotline was flooded with such calls.

One of their major findings is that, in addition to the usual father-daughter and sibling incest found in the West, twenty-nine percent of the Japanese calls complained about mother-son incest. This is an extremely high proportion compared to other countries. But what could be expected considering the common frequency with which Japanese mothers sleep alone with their sons while the father is out having sex with other women. Extramarital sex still is the norm for most married men in Japan (DeMause, 1991). According to other research and interviews in the media, some mothers often offer sexual services to their sons in order to release them from school stress, especially exam stress. The most commonly reported incest occurs when the mother sees her son masturbate as a teenager and tells him, "It's not good to do it alone. Your IQ becomes lower. I will help you." Or, "You cannot study if you cannot have sex. You may use my body." Or, "I don't want you to get into trouble with a girl; have sex with me instead."

The researchers found that Japanese mothers and sons often sleep in the same bed and have sex together although the exact number of occurrences in the population have not been investigated. According to phone interviews, Japanese mothers teach their sons how to masturbate.

Why should these phenomena occur in Japan? I believe there are various explanations for this. First of all, there is the absence of the father and his proper role in the family. This is combined with the role of women and how society views them.

While the father is absent at home and the affairs of the house, it is expected that the mother should care for the kids and run the house. Often, mothers end up in loneliness and this becomes a feeding ground for acts such as mother-son incest.

Secondly, I believe this is due to the frustration of the youth and the stress they have at school and the high level of expectations from family, neighborhoods, schools, etc. This, of course, demands a solution. Since the mother does not know what to do, out of helplessness she commits such acts in order to help her children. We have to be aware that usage of psychological counseling in Japan is low because in Japanese society when someone consults a psychiatrist he or she may lose face in the society. Thus, people avoid calling for clinical help as much as possible.

What happens to the child who experiences this? What is his future? How will that child end up? Is there any link between this and the hikikomori, since hikikomori is predominately a male issue? How many of the hikikomori have had such a terrible experience of incest that they cannot speak about it and, therefore, isolate themselves? Is this hikikomori visualization of extreme Honne reaction that these poor kids not only isolate their minds and their opinions but also their bodies or their entire beings? Or is there any link between suicide of young people and such acts of incest? I think this is a great field for future research. In the meanwhile, I challenge the church in Japan to break taboos by addressing these issues and providing help and organized support for these kids and their mothers. I believe in coming days the church can play an important role in Japan, of course, if the church is willing to do so!

SOCIAL BEHAVIOR CATEGORY

There are also many various phenomena that are not touching the youth, but all the facets of the society touch a wider group of the population. I place this in the category of social behavior. Here are some of these that affect the Japanese society in a negative way.

Gambling and Addiction

Pachinko is a special Japanese gambling machine that is very popular in Japan. There are 20,000 pachinko-halls with an average of 250 machines. The annual income of the pachinko-halls are approximately between 230 to 270 billion U.S. dollars This can be compared with the total GNP of Belgium or even higher than the income of all the Japanese car factories together (Duits, 2002).

There are approximately 1.25 million Japanese who are addicted to Pachinko. The population of Pachinko players and addicts varies. However, the stressed salarymen and single mothers are among these.

Suicide

From 1998–2002 there were more than 30,000 suicide deaths. The rate in Japan is 25 per 100,000. In 2002, 32,143 suicides were reported; this is an increase of 3.5 percent from 2001. In Japan, suicide victims are mostly young adults. Among the age group 15–24 and 40–54, it is the second leading cause of death. In the 25–39 age group it is the leading cause of death. The rate in middle aged men (40–54 years) was five times higher than in women, perhaps because of the association between suicide, unemployment, and economic recession. These days there is an increase in websites that guide their customers step by step through their own deaths.

Finding a Proper Spouse

As the Japanese society is aging, the birth rate is declining. There is an increase in the age when people get married; Japanese youth are struggling to find a proper partner. I have interviewed many youth in Japan, especially girls in their thirties, who are still looking for the right man to marry. Finding a partner in Japan is becoming tougher and tougher. In Japan most of the marriages are arranged through friends and family members. Matchmaking is an old tradition in Japan. However, nowadays it also has become a form of business.

There are organizations especially designed for such activities. They organize dinner nights or other activities to match potential couples. In some clubs, both men and women have to pay a membership fee. In some clubs men do not pay; only women pay for membership.

This is somehow strange, and yet it is understandable when we know that in the Japanese culture as I have discussed before in this book, this is due to the position of women in Japan. In some clubs, women have to pay a membership fee of approximately $3,000 while the men do not pay any membership fee at all.

Some solve their problems by marrying foreigners. Women tend to marry Koreans and men are likely to find their luck and happiness with Chinese, Vietnamese, and especially Filipino women.

Homeless People

The number of homeless people is increasing. They live on the streets, in stations, and public parks and riversides. The number of homeless people in

Tokyo has nearly doubled in the past five years. The average age of Japan's homeless is 55.9 years old. The number of homeless people in Japan is on the rise, and experts say that ingrained cultural attitudes about age are exacerbating the situation. The problem has become so prevalent that Doctors Without Borders — a nongovernmental health organization accustomed to missions in the poorest of nations — sent staff to this hi-tech, high-rise capital (Kambayashi, 2004).

In central Tokyo, the number of homeless nearly doubled to about 6,000 in February 2003 from 3,200 five years ago. A first-ever nationwide survey found 25,296 homeless people in Japan. But the actual number of the homeless is much larger according to those close to the issue. Those from 50 to 64 make up about two-thirds of that population. Moreover, about fifty-five percent of them used to work in construction. Many were day laborers who toiled without fringe benefits to help Japan flourish in the postwar era. But the recession has hit contractors hard (ibid).

In Japan, however, not only the homeless but also those over thirty-five have difficulty finding a job, especially if they are unmarried. Companies expect married men to work more strenuously since husbands here are usually the sole breadwinners. That's why most of the homeless are middle-aged or older single men — a unique aspect of the problem of homelessness in Japan activists say. Most of the homeless are systematically eliminated from society. Japan's homeless problem is attributed to deeply rooted discrimination.

While homeless people suffer from low self-esteem and feelings of inadequacy, age discrimination reinforces their sense of alienation, say those who look after them (ibid).

Lastly

Japanese society is rapidly changing and is facing serious sociological, cultural, and moral challenges. The family situation is strongly under pressure, and women and children belong to a fragile group of the society alongside minorities. Moral illnesses are rapidly expanding and getting more complex in form and shape. Social illnesses such as Hikikomori are one of the few phenomena of the modern high-tech Japanese society. In the following part, I will be analyzing the condition of Japanese society and will come to a conclusion, describing strategies concerning how to reach this nation with the gospel of Jesus Christ as effectively as possible.

Part Five

CONCLUSIONS AND ANALYSIS

CHAPTER

13

ANALYSES AND STRATEGIES

A BRIEF SUMMARY

Japan is a fascinating nation, a society full of mystery and surprises, at least for people who are looking at this nation from a distance, Westerners in particular. In the past twelve chapters, I have described some important aspects of Japan beginning with its formation and theories concerning its origin. I have discussed the historical background, and in particular, the history of Christianity in this nation from the early ages through the formation of modern Japan and contemporary Japan. I explained the commonly accepted theory concerning the origin of the Japanese people, the Jomon people. Also, the mythological origin was discussed which plays an important role in Japanese culture and society.

I did not exclude the theory of Japan being one of the lost tribes of Israel or a mixture of Asian culture and Jewish and Middle Eastern culture. Some festivals were discussed which resembled Jewish customs. In the historical background, the attention went to two major periods: the Tokugawa Period (1603–1868) and the Meiji Period (1868–1912). During the Tokugawa Period, Japan was isolated from the outside world. Except for the Dutch, Japan chose not to cooperate with any other nation, and the society was canalized in classes. The national religion was Buddhism combined with strong Confucian ethics. During this period, Christianity was considered a major threat and was systematically banned. Christians were persecuted and killed publicly. During this period, some Christians managed to keep their faith secretly for a couple of centuries until they were discovered during the Meiji Period.

In Part Two, I focused on the modern Japanese society. Here I described what I believed to be important structural elements of the Japanese society, such as the role of the individual, family, work, gender stratification, minorities, and other important aspects. Also, I discussed some social issues that are threatening the structure of society. These include things like the low birth rate, the fatherless society, and other aspects.

In Part Three, the history of Christianity was described including various theories concerning when and how Christianity entered Japan. The general theory advocates that Christianity came to Japan in the 1500s, yet according to other theories, Christianity entered Japan in earlier centuries. Also, Christianity was described and defined according to what I call non-traditional Christianity. I also looked at the role of the Church and Christianity in Japanese society and the future of the Church in Japan.

In Part Four, I described the Japanese culture and some basic cultural elements such as Honne-Tatemae, Uchi-Soto, Giri, Amae, and Aimai, which were significant for this research and were related to Christianity. They were viewed through the eyes of the Christian faith and how these elements would form a barrier for Christianity to grow in Japan. All these were related to the Christian faith. Also, some socio-cultural problems such as sexual immorality, social protests, suicide, and homelessness in Japan were briefly discussed.

ANALYSES

Japan is a superpower on the edge of moral and social decay. It is a nation searching for answers, a nation without a moral compass. How can the Church play a role in this society and what would be the proper strategies to reintroduce Christianity in Japan?

I personally believe that Christianity has not been introduced properly to Japan. Christianity should be reintroduced in Japan, and the Christian scholars and ministers should prayerfully find new strategies to give Christianity another face. Before discussing some potential strategies for evangelizing Japan, let us first look at some crucial factors of why Christianity has not been growing in Japan. There are several factors concerning this question that can be categorized into three majors factors: the historical factors, the socio-cultural factors, and the church factors.

Historical Factors

First of all, Christianity has been considered a western religion which was from the very beginning connected to the colonialism and imperialism of the 1500s. Already, Christianity was a political threat to Japan. Christianity was considered the religion of the "enemy" that wanted to infiltrate Japan. After the modernization and freedom of religion during the Meiji Period, some Christians made the crucial mistake of entering Japan with their western mindset. They tried to impose the western culture on the Japanese. This, of course, was the second historical factor that blocked Christianity's growth in Japan. Thirdly, after World War II and the defeat of the Japanese by the Americans, including the use of the atomic bomb and the removal of the emperor, the Japanese people disliked Christianity, viewing it as the religion of the Americans who shamefully defeated them.

Cultural Factors

Cultural factors are very crucial. The following are some cultural factors that have blocked the growth of Christianity in Japan. First of all, Shinto, the original Japanese religion, does not promote monotheism. In Japan, the concept of God is totally different than that in the Christian faith. In Japan, gods are considered as neither good nor bad. They are undefined. Gods or kami's are not personal; they do not relate to people. Keep them satisfied and keep them happy and they won't harm you or bring calamities. In Christianity, however, this is the opposite. God is then the supreme creator, kind compassionate, all knowing, and loving. He does not demand religious rites to keep Him happy. He is the God who is full of grace.

The second cultural factor is the concept of sin and the falleness of man. In the Japanese culture, man is by nature good; however, the worldly attachments are bad which make a human corrupt. This can be fought by controlling and minimizing the selfish desires which may result to childishness such as being called a wagamama.

Also, in Japanese, the word used for "sin" is the same as the word used for "crime," and so only a criminal, a thief, or a killer is a "sinner," and not the average Japanese person. In other words, the concept of sin and fallen man is totally different than the biblical doctrine.

When an evangelist tells a Japanese person that he or she is a sinner, the people would not understand because they do not consider themselves as "criminals."

The Japanese are not sin-oriented people, but guilt-oriented people. In the biblical doctrine, however, man is created in the image of God, but since the fall of man there is evil in all persons by nature. Sin is considered as disobeying the Lord's commands and rejecting God's Son as Lord and Savior. This brings us to the third cultural factor, which is the issue of forgiveness. Since there is no proper concept of sin, it is difficult to understand God's forgiveness in the Christian faith. In Japanese culture, if something wrong has been committed, there must be some way to make it good. If there is no way for restitution, then there will be endless shame and guilt not only on that person but also on the family of that person.

In Christianity, however, there is no way of compensation and making good with God. There is only one way and that is through accepting Christ as Lord. He alone can take away any guilt and any shame from us through His grace and mercy.

The number four reason is that the Japanese are group-oriented people. They think in terms of Uchi-Soto, and they have to do all they can for the interests of the group and not their own interests. They do this so they do not lose face with the group which brings dire consequences. For example, the neighborhood in Japan is considered as a form of the uchi group. There are activities including religious activities and duties in every neighborhood. Therefore, if someone begins to attend church he may be considered as a threat to the neighborhood. This will cause shame to the family of the person going to church. This will be more challenging when a person decides to be baptized. Since Japan is a ceremony-oriented nation, baptism may be considered as a betrayal to the national culture of Japan. Therefore, some parents do all they can to stop their newly converted kids from being baptized.

The fifth cultural reason could be that the Japanese consider Christians as childish because Christians claim there is only one way to God — Jesus Christ. This is considered arrogant by the Japanese.

Lastly, the Japanese society is a work-oriented society. Unfortunately, work is more important than family. As I have described earlier in this book, I consider Japan a "company-worshiping" nation. Therefore, church or church activities could reduce a person's loyalty toward the work or company. Since people think that going to church on Sundays makes a person a Christian, people become reluctant to even think about Christianity as their religion because they are afraid to lose the one and only free day they have. Attending church would be an obligation, Giri. There are of course many more factors to be discussed, yet I believe that what I described here is sufficient for our purposes.

Church Factors

By church factors I mean that there are certain responsibilities the Church has towards the changing society. The Church should better represent itself to this rapidly transforming global society, including Japan. I believe, first of all, that there should be a distinction between Church and western culture.

The Church has failed to represent itself as a "culture–free" faith. The Church failed to represent itself as an independent faith. The missionaries and Christians from abroad did not try their best to investigate the nation and the culture in order to build a bridge of trust and understanding. I have interviewed certain believers in Japan and other Asian nations. They consider the western style of Christianity as very aggressive and dominant. Westerners come with the following attitude: "We know better than you and we have come to teach you, the Japanese Christians, something." This is totally against the culture where timidity, silence, calmness, and humbleness play a crucial role.

Another factor is that the Church should relate more to the society and address the current issues in the society. The Church has to offer solutions to various questions and problematic concerns. The Church forms a group and lives a group life on its own. However, the Church should come out of group life and begin to find itself among people. Lastly, the Christian leadership has not kept up with the latest developments in technology, art, and science. This gives the Church an old fashioned and boring image to the average Japanese person. The Church should be closer to the people and society.

STRATEGIES AND SUGGESTIONS

Japan is changing. The position of the family, the youth, the elderly, the educational system, labor management, and the economy are drastically changing and some are undergoing a heavy crisis. In this book I have mentioned some of these crises.

The family is becoming more and more fatherless. Mothers and kids have to find their own way to survive in a merciless and rapidly changing society. As I mentioned before, the way Christianity is growing now in Japan, it will take seven hundred years for Christianity to double its population. The majority of the churches are old fashioned and not current with the rapid developments of technology. Pastors are getting older. Their average age is sixty. Many believe that in twenty years the majority of these churches will be closed down. However, I also mentioned that the Pentecostal and Charismatic forms of Christianity are growing faster. These churches are not many, however, and they can grow and come with new strategies to reach Japan with the gospel of Jesus Christ. In the following paragraphs I will be sharing my suggested strategies for the Church in Japan.

A Total Transformation in Christian Message

Japanese culture is a very complicated set of dualistic contradictions. The Japanese say "yes" but mean "no." They are not able to express their inner feelings in order to keep order in the family or group by being politically correct.

Unfortunately, many Christians in Japan grow up this way, or the society is forcing them or guiding them to be and act this way. Also, faith and belief are individual issues and it is childish or impolite to express your views to someone else.

Cultural elements, such as Honne-Tatemae, Amae or Aimai, remain strongholds. Modern Christianity should address these cultural issues and teach Christians to openly express their ideas and feelings publicly, which is of course against mainstream culture. This means that evangelistic efforts should bypass the limitations of the culture and adopt the culture itself to the Christian message. By doing so, Christians have to find ways to bring the gospel in the private realm of every Japanese. For instance internet has helped the suffering woman to bypass the existing neighborhood culture of control by creating forums online and sharing openly their experiences without loosing face in the neighborhood or in the family. These women often use nicknames and are very open with their inner feelings, which are not easily shared in the normal environment. I was even informed that many women have been helped through such forums, groups and discussion sites. Sending mobile phone or text messages are very effective because many Japanese express their feelings better through texting with mobile phone than by face-to-face interactions.

Can we as Christians use such methods in reaching the Japanese with gospel of Jesus Christ? In order to do so, I believe we have to redefine our understanding of Christianity and church as an organization. I believe that the church as an established organization with buildings, elders, deacons and religious structures will not be able to reach the Japanese people. Therefore, there should be an alternative for new Japanese converts to live out their faith without being expelled from neighborhood communities or families. Will it be possible that postmodern Japanese society will embrace Christianity in a different form, a new way in which technology, social care, and community will play an increasingly important role? Will it be possible to create a community of Japanese Christians who don't have to visit church every Sunday yet are active Christians in the marketplace and society? These are the questions that time will answer. Christianity has a lot to offer during this "compass-less" time in Japan.

Reintroducing Christianity

As I have described in this book, there is a good possibility that Christianity entered Japan long before the western powers introduced their version of the faith. It is important to know that the Church is not only a western faith, but is a faith that came to Asia through the Middle East. The Japanese people should be aware of the potential of their Jewish background or at least discuss the theory in order to bring their hearts closer to the Christian faith so that their view about Christianity being a western religion would change. When the Japanese learned that Christianity entered Japan far earlier than it entered the United Kingdom or the USA, it may have made them think twice about this faith. This could be an open door for interest in Christianity. In my new book *Rediscovering Japan, Reintroducing Christendom: Two Thousand Years of Christian History in Japan* (Hamilton Books), I am describing the rich Judeo-Christian history and culture in Japan. This book will help readers to understand Christianity in Japan's unknown historical background with this faith.

Reaching the Youth

Another strategy for the Church is to reach the youth. But how can the Church reach the youth while the average age of leaders in Japan is sixty years old? The youth are suffering. This comes from suicide, hikikomori, anger and rage against the establishment, bullying, incest, harsh educational system and expectations, and youth prostitution.

The youth need help to come out of their crisis. There are websites guiding the youth to commit suicide. The majority of the churches do not offer deep and effective outreach to these youth. My suggestion is that the churches should start digital solutions and campaigns in reaching the youth.

Strong Internet services are needed to reach the Japanese youth. Websites, forums, and chatting services should create an atmosphere of providing a helping hand.

Another crisis of the youth is finding a proper spouse. Due to the aging society and the low birthrate, Japanese youth have a problem finding partners. I believe the Church can play a crucial role of Christian Miai, or Christian matchmaking agencies.

Reaching Minorities and Immigrants

As I have mentioned in this book, the minorities such as the Burakumin and other minority groups are strongly being discriminated against. These minorities have a Japanese background and yet they are not considered as Japanese. I believe the Church should find proper strategies and services to reach these minorities. As I have done my research and some informal talks with some Japanese Christians, I have discovered that there are even prejudices within the Christian Church. Even the Christians do not like to interact with people such as the Burakumin. Even Christian parents do not like their children to marry Christians with a Burakumin or Ainu background.

The Christians in Japan should open helping arms to these minorities. From the other side there are non-Japanese minorities such as the Koreans. The church is very strong among the Korean community in Japan. Koreans have bigger churches than the average Japanese church. Therefore, supporting the Korean church in Japan and the Korean missionaries in Japan would be very effective since the negative image of Koreans in Japan is beginning to change.

More and more Japanese women are getting married to Korean men, so the church can use this opportunity to expose the Japanese women to the gospel of Jesus Christ. Also, other minorities such as Filipinos are also very active in Japan, establishing their fellowships and Christian community. Nowadays, international churches are getting more and more in Japan. These are churches with mixed nationalities — Filipinos, Chinese, and Koreans.

There are also Japanese and Africans, etc. Interaction between the Japanese Christians and other Christian nationalities can create a good atmosphere of unity and preparation in reaching Japan with the gospel.

Women, the Secret for Revival in Japan

By now, it may already be clear that the position of women in Japan is not well. Many women in Japan are suffering; many go through loneliness, pain, and the frustrations of the society. Also, culturally they are not viewed as equal to men even though the law says so! Women have become a spotlight of sexual pleasures, sexual maltreatments, etc.

Therefore, the Church should change its doctrine about women. It may sound strange, but in Japan women attend church more than men. However, these women in the Church are trained traditionally to keep silent and only come to church for their own personal worship. The attitude of the Church towards Japanese women should be changed. There is an old saying, "iron sharpens iron." Once the Japanese women, old and young, are set free, respected, and being released into Christian service in boldness, then they will offer solutions and counseling to many women in Japan who are looking for answers and solutions.

The Christian community in Japan should reform its point of view about women in the Church, and Christian women should be encouraged to break the cultural barriers such as Honne-Tatemae, Giri, etc. The Christian women in Japan should be effectively trained and released into evangelism and counseling.

CLOSING REMARKS

We should never forget the blood of the martyrs shed on the Japanese soil. We also have to remember the courage of many Christians who kept their faith in secret for almost three hundred years during the Tokugawa Period. I also believe that the current church should do more and ask forgiveness from God and from the Japanese people for apathy and ignorance about the things developing in the society. We should be asking forgiveness for not being a part of this society and not attempting enough to offer solutions and care for this desperate people. I believe that by keeping and practicing what I just discussed in this book alongside carefully and strategically praying for Japan, the hearts of the Japanese people will be more open and receptive to our message. This will surely lead to a revival of the Christian faith in this nation. One has to love Japan in order to reach Japan.

I am aware of certain criticisms from my Christian colleagues who would ask me why I did not address things such as spiritual warfare and demonology of the Japanese gods. I am well aware of these matters, and I intentionally chose not to address them. I simply want this book to be a Christian sociological book, which will be used as a handbook and an eye opener for every person and every Christian missionary, evangelist, or pastor who wants to reach this beautiful nation with love of Christ and not with a western religion!

BIBLIOGRAPHY

BENEDICT, Ruth (1946) The Chrysanthemum and the Sword: patterns of Japanese culture. Boston: Houghton Mifflin Company.

BEST, Ernest (1966) Christian faith and cultural crisis: the Japanese case. Leiden: Brill.

BOWRING, Richard & KORNICKI, Peter (1993) The Cambridge Encyclopedia of Japan. Cambridge: Cambridge University Press.

CRAWCOUR, Sydney (1974) The Tokugawa period and Japan's preparation for modern economic growth. The Journal of Japanese Studies: 1(1): 113–125.

CURTIN, J. Sean (2005) Women and Japan's new poor, article written for www.japanfocus.org

DAVIS, Roger & IKEDO, Osamu (2002) The Japanese mind: understanding contemporary Japanese culture. Boston: Tuttle Publishing.

DeMAUSE, Lloyd (1991) The Universality of incest. (Article) New York: the Journal of Psychohistory 19 (2), winter 1991.

DUITS, Kjeld (2002) Vrouw breekt los: de vele gezichten van Japan. Translation from Dutch: woman breaks loose: many faces of Japan. The Hague: Uitgeverij BZZToH.

DZIESINSKI, Michael J. (2003) Hikikomori: investigations into the phenomenon of acute social withdrawal in contemporary Japan (paper). Honolulu: University of Hawaii, Manoa.

FRANCE-PRESSE, Agence (1998).

FRANCIS, Carolyn Bowen & NAKAJIMA, John Masaaki (1991) Christians in Japan. New York: Friendship Press, Inc.

HALL, John Whitney (1991) Japan: prehistory to modern times. Frankfurt am Main: S. Fischer Verlag.

HARRINGTON, Ann M. (1993) Japan's hidden Christians. Chicago: Loyola University Press.
HENDRY, Joy (2004) Understanding Japanese society. London: Routledge Curzon.
HIGASHIBABA, Ikuo (2001) Christianity in early modern Japan: Kirishitans belief & practice. Leiden: Brill.
IMAMURA, Anne E. (1990) The Japanese family article written for the Asian Society's Video Letter from Japan II: a young family, pages 7–17.
JENKINS, Philip (2003) The Rise of Global Christianity: a Conversation with Philip Jenkins & David Brooks. Washington CD: Ethics and Public Policy Center.
JOHNSTONE, Patrick & MANDRIJK Jason (2001) Operation world: 21st century edition. Carlisle, UK: Paternoster Lifestyle.
JOSEPH, Ken Jr. (2001) Lost identity. Tokyo: The Keikyo Institute.
KAMBAYASHI, Takehiko (2004) Japan's homeless face ageism (article, 18 October 2004) The Christian Science Monitor (www.scmonitor.com)
KATAYAMA, Patricia Mari (Editor) (2004) Talking about Japan: Q&A. Third Edition. Tokyo: Bilingual Books.
KUBO, Arimasa (1999) Lost tribes-Japan: Israelites came to Japan. Tokyo: Remnant Publishing.
LANDE, Aasulv (1989) Meiji Protestantism in history and historiography. Frankfurt am Main: Verlag Peter Lang GmbH.
LEBRA, T. Sugiyama (1976) Japanese patterns of behavior. Honolulu: University of Hawaii Press.
LEE, Samuel (2008) Blessed Migrants: God's strategy for global revival. Amsterdam: SLWE.
LEE, Shiu Keung (1971) The cross & the lotus. Hong Kong: Christian Study Center on Chinese Religion and Culture.
LEWIS, R.D. (1996) When culture collide: managing successfully across cultures. London: Nicholas Brealey.
MACNEIL, David (2003) Sexy and smart: one sector that won't be left behind: Japan's massive sex industry has shifted from bricks-and-mortar deflation to Internet elation — Industry Overview An internet article in (www.findarticles.com)
MASAKO, Ishii-Kuntz (du*) Japanese fathers' involvement in childcare, a power point presentation. (*du = date unknown) University of California, Riverside: department of sociology.
MCDOWELL, Josh (1994) Christianity: a ready defense. San Bernardino: Here's Life Publishing Inc.

MEYVIS, Ludo & VANDE WALLE, Willy (1989) Japan: het onvoltooide experiment. Translation from Dutch: (Japan: the unfinished experiment). Tielt: Drukkerij-Uitgeverij Lanno, Belgium.

MONI, Monir Hossain (2004) Christianity's Failure to Thrive in Today's Japan (paper) Tokyo: Hitotsubashi University, Dept. of International and Asia- Pacific Studies.

NAKANE, Chie (1973) Japanese society. California: University of California Press.

NAOFUSA, Hirai (1987) Shinto in Eliade Micrea (ed.), the encyclopedia of religion. New York: Macmillan Publishing Co.

OLIAI, MH (1997) Japanese ethic and the road to development (paper.). Leiden: University of Leiden.

ROHLEN, Thomas P. (1974) For harmony and strength: Japanese white-color organization in anthropological perspective. Berkley: University of California Press.

REISCHAUER, Edwin O. & CRAIG, Albert M (1978) Japan: tradition & transformation. Rutland: Vermont and Tokyo.

STORM, Stephanie (2000) Japan slowly embraces greater income inequality over social harmony. Article in New York Times, January 4, 2000.

SUGIMOTO, Yoshio (2002) An Introduction to Japanese Society. Cambridge: Cambridge University Press.

TAKIMOTO, Jun (2005) The day the Lord arose, Shinshiro, Japan: All Revival Mission.

THANG, Leng Leng (2002) Touching of the hearts: an overview of programs to promote interaction between the generations in Japan, in R. Goodman (ed.), Family and social policy in Japan: anthropological approaches. Cambridge: Cambridge University Press.

WOJTAN, Linda S. (2000) Exploring contemporary Japanese society. Japan Digest: www.japandigest.com

Interesting Websites

Aids Education Global Information System
www.aegis.com

Answers Fast Facts
www.answers.com

Asian Access Japan
www.asianaccess.org

Christian Examiner Online: Gallup poll of Japan finds Christian on the upswing, May 2006 www.christianexaminer.com

Contemporary Japan
http://afe.easia.columbia.edu/at_japan_soc/common/all.htm

Gospel Japan
www.gospeljapan.com

Human Rights Documentation Center
www.hrdc.net

Israelites came to Japan:
http://www5.ocn.ne.jp/~magi9/isracam2.htm

Japan Focus
www.japanfocus.org

Japan Guide Online resources
www.japan-guide.com

Japan Evangelical Missionary Alliance
www.jema.org

Keikyo: the Japan Christian Internet Address
www.keikyo.com

Mission Japan
www.missionjapan.com

Religious Tolerance
www.religioustolerance.org

Web Japan: Gateway for all the Japanese information
http://web-japan.org

FORTHCOMING ...

"*Rediscovering Japan, Reintroducing Christendom: Two Thousand Years of Christian History in Japan*" looks at Japan and its unvoiced Christian history and cultural roots from an alternative perspective. It is commonly believed that Christianity was introduced to Japan by the Spanish/Portuguese missionaries during the 1500s. Samuel Lee however, draws on various forms of cultural, religious and linguistic evidence to argue that Christianity was introduced to Japan through the Lost Tribes of Israel, who were converted to Christianity through the missionary efforts of the Assyrian Church of the East around A.D. 500. Much of the evidence he discusses has become submerged into many Japanese folkloric songs, festivals and is to be found in temples. There are, for example, approximately 300 words in Japanese and Hebrew/Aramaic that are similar. Further, Dr. Lee outlines the history of Catholicism in Japan during the 1500s, the systematic persecution of Christians from 1600s to the 1800s and the rise of Protestant Church in Japan. The historical portion of the book ends with an analysis and discussion of 21st century Japanese society. Lastly, in *Rediscovering Japan, Reintroducing Christendom*, Samuel Lee questions the missiological methods of Western Christianity and advocates an approach based in dialogue between Christianity and other cultures.

For more information or ordering this book visit www.univpress.com or email the author directly at samuel.lee@foundationuniversity.com

Foundation University Japan Project
www.projectjapan.org

www.ingramcontent.com/pod-product-compliance
Lightning Source LLC
LaVergne TN
LVHW051833080426
835512LV00018B/2850